The Venice Collection

GLORAFILIA

The Venice Collection

---

25 original projects in needlepoint and embroidery

CAROLE LAZARUS and JENNIFER BERMAN

CONRAN OCTOPUS

Dedicated to our parents,
who first introduced us to Venice

Project Editor Patsy North *Art Director* Mary Evans
Copy Editor Penny David *Art Editor* Alison Fenton
Picture Research Nadine Bazar *Design Assistant* Alison Barclay
Production Jackie Kernaghan *Illustrator* Paul Bryant

Special Photography Bill Batten
Studio Photography David Gill
Montages Karen Bowen
Location Stylist Sue Skeen

* * *

First published in 1991 by
Conran Octopus Limited
37 Shelton Street
London WC2H 9HN

British Library Cataloguing in Publication Data
Lazarus, Carole
    Glorafilia: the Venice Collection: 25 original projects
    in needlepoint and embroidery
    1. Embroidery
    I. Title   II. Berman, Jennifer
    746.44

ISBN 1 85029 340 6

Typeset by Medcalf Type Ltd, Bicester, Oxon
Printed and Bound in China

Contents

INTRODUCTION
6

VENETIAN TEXTILES
12

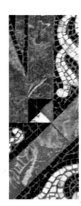

DECORATIVE VENICE
34

BACKSTREETS AND BACKWATERS
56

VENICE AND FOOD
74

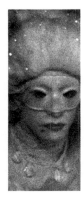

CARNIVAL
94

CRAFTS AND CHARACTERS
116

INTRODUCTION

INTRODUCTION

Why Venice? Because, not to put too fine a point on it, we are both besotted with, passionate about and obsessed by the city! Venice has been an inspiration for writers, musicians, artists, designers for centuries . . . but needlework? Rarely. And when Venice itself is a tapestry – a magical marriage of past magnificence and present kitsch, stone and water, sound and smell, indivisibly dissolving into each other, it seems time to redress the balance.

We have used Venetian themes we love, some obvious, some that made us catch our breath in surprise. You can do the same, with Venice, or with any other city. With a photograph or a memory, a handful of yarns, some canvas or linen, a deep breath and a little confidence, let the imagination fly – needlework is so subtle we can interpret whatever we choose. Water – let's use silks, stranded and mixed . . . mosaics – metallic threads and flat cottons . . . stonework – wool in structured stitches, building up textures. Play and experiment – add, unpick, repeat – until your canvas pinpoints the core of what excited you. The final piece of work will be far more telling than any photograph could be. Look at the mosaics on pages 34 and 35. Now look more closely. So many nuances will appear that at first are unnoticed. You don't need to be able to draw. Make an abstraction – random spontaneous stitching can communicate more enjoyment than a formal study. The best work we do, with the most life in it, is done as an indulgence, unselfconscious and unrestricted.

There were two prerequisites for writing this book. The first was a love affair we have both had with Venice since childhood, perhaps when the irreversible seeds were planted, on the basis of 'stay long enough in one place and your footsteps stay forever in the sand' – or in this case, on marble or mosaic. It is the unconditional love with which one regards an eccentric favourite aunt. The impressionable child, the romantic adolescent, the only slightly more realistic adult mind have all been imprinted with images, echoes, fragments etched into head and heart with an indelible quill. And when D.H. Lawrence speaks of 'an abhorrent, green, slippery city', we agree, with 'Yes, isn't it glorious!'

The second requirement was the room. We converted a tiny corner of The Old Mill House, where the door could be closed, the phone unplugged and the space used to beckon whatever we wanted to conjure up. Over the months the room changed from anonymous white plaster to a magnificent mix of canvas, wool, silk, textiles, prints, photographs – literally a tapestry, of time and texture. The shelves and floor vanished and were replaced by myriads of colours. While Glorafilia continued along its Victorian Garden path, behind the closed door some alchemy was happening, the room tilted towards the fifteenth century, we turned our backs on the trees outside our rural window and hideous world events, and became entwined in a city of Gothic and Byzantine imagery, shimmering *palazzi*, damp backstreets brushed by shadows in black capes and tricorn hats. We started in April and ended at Christmas. The only visible reference to the twentieth century was the word processor; the rest was like an attic of treasures, the opening of a chest filled with rainbow brocades, rich damasks, tassels and whispers of past lives.

Venice is so familiar from film and paint that at first sight it seems impossibly fictitious. You may absorb facts and dates, go armed with preconceived perceptions and lots of information, but will it help you feel the essence of the city, do these facts tell us anything about the pulse of Venice? The best thing initially is to forget guidebooks, sit in cafés, walk the alleyways and let Venice seep into you through the soles of your feet. In a place of such indelibility, the mind can become a theatre of images and the unsuspecting heart is lost.

Venice presents herself like a galleon in full sail, with the ostentation of a peacock, yet at the same time making such a poignant statement about the twentieth century. On each visit we see something new, many things new – because although Venice changes very little, we change a lot. When we were thinking about this book, we saw a familiar columned doorway at the Church of the Frari which we'd never noticed in the same way before: twisting barley-sugar marble shapes that an artist would itch to draw, a writer to describe, but to us they begged to be translated into textured stitching, silky threads, silver glints, dull knotted shadows. It takes a little practice, because we are all used to observing and absorbing a scene as a whole and for needlework we need to edit and look for detail. And Venice is made for that. In general and in particular, it is a visual feast of glorious images tumbling . . . slivers of ancient glass beads, stonework crumbling into water, amber sunshine on the fantasy architecture. This book is to share our love for a city, and we hope to open doors to seeing with 'needlework' eyes.

* * *

We have actually spent more time together in Venice than with families, husbands, other friends. We first got to know each other on a Greek ship from Venice, travelling steerage. That was in the sixties when we painted freckles on our faces and had shipboard romances with people who had names like Nikos and Costas. We have been in Venice through the days of stiletto heels and can-can petticoats, Existentialist black, prim gabardine, barefoot in Afghan ethnic, jangling like goats; we have gone from the extremes of transparent voile to Anna Karenina furs, Che Guevara battledress to classic French. We have been severely poor and superbly extravagant, each appreciated more because of the other. We have breakfasted standing in a backstreet café, deciding which bread we could afford, and we have also breakfasted in the divine lunacy of a flower-filled terrace of a Grand Canal *palazzo*, though not on the same day. And we now know that what the French call a 'certain age' brings Comfortable Shoes and an American Express Card.

As with most friendships over so many years, we have drawers stuffed with shared memories, many of them labelled Venice. While researching this book, we made a sentimental journey to the Lido. The season hadn't yet started, the sand was banked up from the winter and those silent elegant beaches were being

prepared for the coming summer. We walked symbolically from the public beach at the bottom of the Gran Viale, to No. 1 *cabana* on the Excelsior beach. Over the years we used both, and nowadays would choose neither, unless it was October and the crowds had gone. We reminisced about sybaritic summers before Responsibility entered our lives, giggling over the director at the film festival, each of us with one of his podgy hands pressing an innocent knee, about our near escapes, parties, fireworks. We looked for Beppino's record shop, which wasn't there; the house which let rooms, which was; and for Ondina's family villa.

As years went on, either together or separately, we spent less time on the Lido and more time in the city, and made it the scenery for many milestones: a honeymoon, fortieth birthdays, anniversaries, any excuse will actually do for a dinner at Harry's, a lunch at the Locanda in Torcello – and in between any excuse will actually do as well: drawing lessons (children seated on chilly stones before breakfast, hating their mother, but Learning to Draw), business trips that slid off the mainland, short cultural bouts, prolonged uncultural bouts. We both view it as a bolt-hole of enormous magnetism, repetition somehow increasing the pleasure like the familiarity of special friends, the place we most enjoy being. We visualize ourselves in arthritic old age, supporting each other's frail limbs up and down the little bridges, still bickering over which café serves the best chocolate croissant, future generations coming to pay duty visits to their grandmothers, blissfully rotting in tune to the rotting city.

* * *

Our present-day bodies are not designed for Venice. Here in London we drive cars, sit in offices, occasionally pedal an exercise bike, have meals at mealtimes. There we walk up and down bridges, across *campi*, along *calli*, either with an approximate destination or just meandering, admiring the magic. Venice is for *dolce far niente*, doing sweet nothing, stopping all the time for: just an espresso, or perhaps a little something sugary/biscuity/stuffed with ricotta and spinach; perhaps just one of those little sandwiches (the *tramezzini* that lodge permanently on the thighs) full of Russian salad and papery layers of ham; saying to each other, to our children, to our men, isn't it time for a little something oozing *crème patissière*, or an apricot juice, a foaming *cappuccino* just before this bridge, just after this bridge; or a little tea over there, a little martini at Harry's? Without such stops the legs shriek at the threat of one more flight of stairs, the top floor of one more ancient *palazzo*, to peer in the gloom at one more fragment of brocade.

The seventeenth-century *palazzetto* where we rent an apartment has walls covered in faded silk that moves at whim, undulating the mirrors that hang against it. The floors slope, a tide of marble; the ancient furniture has three out of four legs balanced on wooden blocks, and with the canal below shimmering reflection into the room the sensation is of living on a boat. We are woken by chiming bells, ardent pigeons being repelled by their ladies, voices calling, always voices calling in Venice,

and sleep to the sound of other bells, different voices echoing and an accordion somewhere on the canals perpetually playing 'Granada'. A woodworm, competing in the Woodworm Grand Prix, hourly leaves such impressive chewings that we expect one morning to find the dining table a pile of sawdust. Across the hall is a tiny frescoed chapel, almost large enough for two, dripping angels and clouds and where Maria-Grazia rests the laundry. The ground floor, now damp and unused, was once the watergate entrance for gondolas. As in Venice generally, the residents retreat roofwards.

Within this apartment alone, we could find a dozen themes to explore with needle and thread. The floor is the colour of rich fruit cake made of mottled marble. The ceilings are swirling classical frescoes in pink and grey. The shutters peel and the paint has a patina almost iridescent. Ivy and antirrhinums grow from the crevices of the house a few feet across the canal, a flaking iron balcony, the ubiquitous geraniums and cats . . . the brickwork is twenty shades of yellow and terracotta. Each of these images seems to dictate for itself the different yarns that could be used, the size and type of stitch, whether to make a picture, cushion or tiny scrap of needlework to be appliquéd to a piece of antique fabric. Once we start thinking 'needlework', new doors open in the way we look at things.

* * *

The Venetians call themselves the curators of their strange museum, as time continues to ravage. The rest of us come to trample and stare and think we are the first to accept the quirks and irritations. Beneath the glitz, the Sunday bells, the razzmatazz of a showpiece, is a weary courtesan whose glamour flakes and whose dignity keeps her re-applying the make-up, in spring gathering herself for another season, in winter abandoned by the masses and resting as the icy fogs sweep up the Adriatic. And, on cold ghostly November nights, is it possible to use the life-saving words 'Please call me a cab'? No. We are condemned to scurry the dark streets, bundled like Eskimos.

But . . . but . . . we know of nothing to compare with the sound of Venetian rain. To lie in bed and listen to it on the canal outside is like being surrounded by a thousand trickling waterfalls.

There are several ways to arrive in Venice – gone are the days of the Grand Tour, and for most of us with time restrictions this means travelling by plane. From the tarmac one sees far-off towers and silhouettes and then travels by boat past numerous channel markers and tumbling reed island houses, past San Michele and its magnificent cypresses (Giorgio tells us why cemeteries grow cypresses, triumphantly translating *radici* (roots) directly into his charming English: 'because their radishes grow straight down!') and into Venice through a back door. The city starts abruptly, not as we would enter a city by road. Imagine a walled citadel, with a sea moat. The boat slides between the buildings of the tradesmen's entrance, rather than the elegance of the front door, the motors cut and we glide in mellow early evening through the looking-glass into Wonderland.

The first time, the first sight of the city should be either by sea across the lagoon, or arriving by train. Crossing the causeway from the mainland and seeing Venice rising from the water with impossibly modest theatricality, her face turned seaward, is never forgotten, and renews itself with each visit. The first sight of New York across the water is not dissimilar, but New York seems dropped from the sky, whereas Venice is born from the sea. It is what Shelley called 'fabrics of enchantment piled to heaven'. And if New York is breathtaking that first time, with Venice one is permanently out of breath. To walk down the station steps in the tumult of travellers and commuters disgorging on to the Grand Canal and its amazing backdrop of architecture is like a slap around the face, reminding the disbelieving visitor that yes, storybooks can be real. In theory, one should arrive like Garbo, the walk to the *motoscafo* being smoothed by unseen hands. In practice, there is bartering with the water-taxi driver, or queueing and struggling, waiting and pushing, to get on to the correct *vaporetto*. But when you do . . . how satisfying is the feeling of corroded iron railings and the grinding and churning of metal and water to someone beginning a life-long passion for a city.

While on passion: it is said that 'no young woman should go to Venice without her lover'. Now we no longer classify ourselves as young women, we have amended it to 'no woman should go to Venice without her lover'. Is this really necessary?

Granted, it helps to be in love anywhere; even the bleakest, greyest, dreariest, dullest would take on quite a glow seen through those particular intoxicated eyes, but with Venice . . . it is extra icing on an already excessive gâteau. There are definitely comparisons to be made between love and Venice. With Venice, too, the normal point of reference is moved sideways, the mind and heart are bombarded with new bubbles of surprise and contradiction. Can there be anywhere more of a fantasy, more frivolous, more seductive, more adored – more fickle, irrational, irritating, inconsistent – more lonely, sad, brave, more changeable, more dignified? More pompous, more elegant, more theatrical, more ostentatious. More betrayed? At first we may be entranced by the façade, the face the city presents, and then like any relationship the flaws begin, the complexities and weaknesses. We have to see beyond, to the essence. Oh yes, Venice in love is truly the stuff of which memories are made, and we should diligently collect these things when we are younger, in the hope that when we are older we can still pair the faces with the names! Whatever, on approaching middle-aged practicality we made a further amendment to that saying – 'No woman should go to Venice without her lover and her needlepoint.'

Opposite and above: Gateways lead to hidden courtyards and entrances, tantalizing the imagination.
Top: Arches in Piazza di San Marco with their elaborate festooned blinds.

VENETIAN TEXTILES

VENETIAN TEXTILES

In 1271 Marco Polo joined his father and uncle on a voyage to the Orient via Acre, Persia and the Gobi Desert. From these journeys they brought back home to Venice more than fantastic stories, they brought textiles from China where silk weaving was a thousand years old and where 'rich men dress in cloth of gold, silk and rich skins, the most beautiful jerkins in the world made from camel hide and goldcloth and beautiful shawls and gilded skins'. This was an important beginning for Venice: the marriage between skills acquired from the Oriental weavers and the creativity and taste of the Italians, which combined to produce cloth from which a whole industry and trade developed, and which was to be imprinted on the style and image of the Venetians for centuries.

To produce fabrics to perfection, the silk passed through sixteen pairs of hands. Until the fourteenth century, to safeguard this art, every master, mistress and workperson was forbidden to work his craft outside Venice. Venetian dyers learnt new methods by attracting experts from other towns, with new techniques and exotic recipes, for example this unappetizing one for black dye:

25oz lye soap
12oz rock-alum left in lumen 24 hrs
110oz galls for mordanting, left 36 hrs
30oz vitriol
12oz gum arabic
12oz iron filings
8oz antimony
3oz sugar

We would add two footnotes: firstly, wear rubber gloves; and secondly, item 3 is not recommended as a substitute when making chopped liver.

Street names indicate where the dyeing houses were: Calle del Verde (Green Lane), Calle dei Colori (Lane of Colours), Campiello del Scarlatto (Scarlet Square). One description reads: 'a twisted lane, serpentine, indeed called the Lane of the Snake, in whose coils here and there are scattered workshops in which one may gaze on every piece of weaving equipment in the city and a scarcely credible number of craftsmen, occupied in the fashioning of gold and variously coloured silks'.

By the seventeenth century Venice was losing commercial power and the weaving production was reduced; from other parts of Europe came the need for luxurious goods which still only Venetians with their magnificent traditions could satisfy. But Venice resisted new mechanization, which was revolutionizing the industry, and her decline was rapid, though the requirements of the Venetians themselves were still met, provided – this quote is from a curious contemporary statistic – that men and women *civili* (refined) contented themselves with one dress, one cloak, one mask per person, and men and women *mediocre* (common) contented themselves with half a dress, half a cloak and half a mask per person.

The nineteenth century brought an atmosphere of further decline in the textile industry, attributed to the competition from Florence, Vicenza, Milan and from France. The spectacular velvets, once so famous, were almost forgotten. The only factory left in 1858 had six looms and struggled on, producing 'such distinct workmanship that it need not fear competition from French velvets'. As time went on, certain trades recovered, Rubelli's fabric production being one and the establishment of Michelangelo Jesurum's lace workshop being another – more about the lace industry a little later.

In a world today of faster, higher, bigger, we cling more and more to the antidote: the slow, the meticulously small, the laborious detail. At Glorafilia we find ourselves involved in noise, speed, computers, fax and phone, paper by the ton, canvas by the kilometre, wool by the sheepload, and the essence of what we really do can easily become secondary. What we really do is coax threads into curves and rainbows and painstakingly experiment with mixing two threads of cotton plant with three threads of silkworm, and mauve instead of grey, and building up images. It is the fundamental fascination of what can be created from disparate elements – and in this we can all be master chefs taking unlikely ingredients and

creating beautiful things. It is for this reason that we are drawn to the Venetians keeping alive precious old traditions, truly as a labour of love – traditions using ancient techniques and formulae which yield stunning results.

At Rubelli, craftsmen still practise cherished ways to produce lengths of embossed velvets, *velluti soprarizzi*, at less than a metre a day, and in these days of automation, the image of fabric unwinding like a snail's trail is a joy. And also explains why, when we lust after Rubelli fabrics in Venice and London, we also shudder at the prices. We photographed in the Rubelli *palazzo* so had lots of time to shudder and lust . . .

There are several tiny companies who use techniques similar to those used by Mariano Fortuny to produce handblock-printed silk velvets, inspired by antique Venetian and Oriental motifs. The stunning effects do not come easily. They require patience and precision; each design element is carefully carved on a small wooden block and the formulae are kept secret. If the fabrics are a wonder – each superseding the next, sliding through unfamiliar fingers like fluid – the clothes are a fantasy: rippling turbans and cloaks and gathered robes. Had Titania and Oberon lived in Venice, this is what they would have

worn. In the Tassels and Purple Brocade projects on pages 22 and 27, we want to show the opulence of those beautiful damasks that are still associated with Venice today, not only in their look, but in all they suggest of glories past.

Opposite: Fragment from an eighteenth-century stole.
Above: Painting by Longhi of a tailor: Il Sarto.
Below: Embroidered shoes from the Correr Museum.

Up to the eighteenth century, embroidery was done mainly in religious institutions and orphanages, and by spinsters and people on probation. Needlework was also taught to aristocratic families, by men, and there are charming etchings of girls transferring designs from a chart, using either the light from a window or a candle placed behind the fabric to help them with their tracing.

Embroidery really came into its own in the eighteenth century — up to then the weaving of elaborate materials took so long that they were considered a symbol of power and wealth, and embroidery, which was quicker, was seldom used by the nobility. However, when easier ways of making cloth were found, weaving became less prestigious. The Venetian playwright Goldoni said of cloth: 'It no longer lasts twenty years, it doesn't weigh on my shoulders, it is inferior, all I have to do is pass near someone and my clothes will be ruined!' So embroidery began . . . and what embroidery! Waistcoats with herons feeding wolves, great feathery flowers, pouched bags with metallic posies, taffeta hats with trailing roses, silk mittens, exotic purses worked with spiralling beads, coats — such as the one we have copied as a waistcoat — decorated with great sprays of iris, rose and auricula, gilets embroidered with scalloped waves to imitate lace, shoes scattered with summer sprigs, or with Dorothy Parker's single perfect rose.

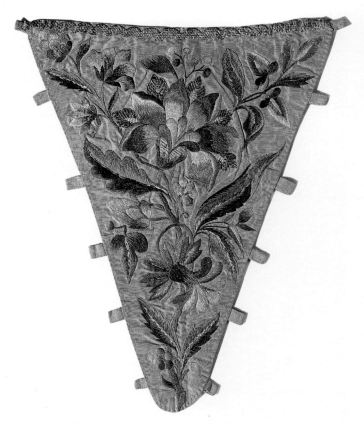

The flower panels used in our Yellow Panel project opposite came from an embroidered dress bodice worked around 1740. The original is in yellow silk, embroidered in silk and spun silver. It would be very hard to improve on the original, so we have worked the stitches as faithfully as we can; the colours and design are a delight, and the only creative licence we have taken is to substitute gold thread for the silver. The eye becomes imprinted with such excess and abundance — if we wore such clothes today, imagine how differently life would be conducted!

Another Venetian innovation took place in the nineteenth century. Places other than Venice started producing their own glass, so the Venetians had to find a new use for their glass and embroidered glass beadwork was introduced (and quickly adopted by the French and English to produce the beautiful subtle examples we seem unable to achieve today). The Venetians, not restricted to drawing-room roses, worked umbrellas, bedspreads, an entire theatre curtain, the canopy at San Zanipolo, all with glass beads, on the basis of 'if a thing is worth doing . . . .

Our minds saturated with glorious images of the romantic eighteenth and nineteenth centuries, we looked for sleek opulent embroidered waistcoats for our unsleek twentieth-century men, and failed.

Left: Longhi's portrait of lawyer Luigi Pisani's family — informally gathered for Sunday brunch.
Above: The original dress bodice, worked around 1740, which inspired our embroidered panels shown opposite.

YELLOW PANEL

We have shown this cushion panel used singly and as a pair. It was inspired by a bodice embroidered in silk and metallic thread around 1740. We have imitated the original stitches and added some new ones — and have used gold thread instead of the original spun silver.

Finished size of design
11.5 × 28.5cm (4½ × 11¼in)

Yarns
Quantity given is for one panel
Appleton's crewel wool

877
pale peach
1 skein

741
blue
1 skein

705
peach
1 skein

342
olive
1 skein

204
terracotta
1 skein

831
emerald
2 skeins

206
rust
1 skein

302
fawn
1 skein

885
lilac
1 skein

Penelope lurex thread

gold
1 card

DMC coton perlé No.5

676
gold
5 skeins

Canvas
18-gauge white interlock
Size: 20 × 37cm (8 × 14½in)

Other materials
Tapestry needle, size 22
Ruler or tape measure
Masking tape for binding the canvas
Sharp scissors for cutting the canvas
Embroidery scissors
Sharp HB pencil or fine permanent
   markers in suitable colours
Eraser

Marking the canvas
Cut the canvas to size and bind the edges with masking tape. Trace the outline (from page 150) on to the canvas with a pencil or permanent marker, centring the tracing. Follow the curved lines freely, ignoring the canvas grid. When tracing straight lines, use your discretion and mark the outline on the closest thread.

If you are experienced it is not necessary to trace the fine lines, which are a guide to show where the colours on the flowers and leaves change. These fine lines can be disregarded or can be put on afterwards, freehand, in a different colour. A beginner may need to trace the fine lines – do this in a different colour after you have traced the thick lines.

Stitches used

TENT stitch (1)
SATIN stitch (3)
SPLIT BACK stitch (6)
LONG AND SHORT stitch (7)
For stitch instructions, see pages 144 and 145.

Stitching the design

Use the whole thread of coton perlé for the background. Use the whole thread of gold lurex in the highlights on the stems and leaves. Use two strands of crewel wool everywhere else on the design.

The numbers on the coloured artwork refer to the stitch numbers. Refer to the photograph of the made-up cushion and the coloured artwork to show you which colour goes where. Remember, this is a guide; don't be restricted by it, and feel free to experiment.

Begin by working the flowers in LONG AND SHORT stitch (7). The buds are in SATIN stitch (3), some outlining is in SPLIT BACK stitch (6) and the small flowers are in TENT stitch (1). The leaves are in SATIN stitch (3) and LONG AND SHORT stitch (7). The stems and veins are in SPLIT BACK stitch (6). The gold highlights on the flowers and leaves are in diagonal SATIN stitch (3). The background is sewn in TENT stitch (1) in gold coton perlé.

Making up instructions

When the design has been sewn, the needlepoint may need to be stretched back into shape (see stretching instructions on page 139). Then make it up into a cushion with a panel as shown on page 140. Alternatively, you may wish to frame the panel and we suggest you take it to a professional picture framer who will also stretch it for you.

Above: Photographed in Contessa Maria Franchin's palazzo on the Grand Canal, the waistcoat was inspired by a man's coat, elaborately embroidered in silk around 1790.

Opposite: The Tassels cushion — a design typical of the richness of Venetian textiles — opulent tassels strewn across damask in characteristic mellow colours.

TASSELS

Elaborate tassels thrown across damask evoke the opulence of Venetian textiles. The colours are typical of those used in fourteenth-century Venice. The damask is worked in wool and shaded cotton in tent stitch to allow the stitching on the tassels to predominate. These are worked mainly in stem stitch, following the flow of the tassel.

Finished size of design
28cm (11in) square

Yarns
Appleton's tapestry wool
75cm (30in) lengths

 302
brown
108 lengths

Anchor stranded cotton

369
cinnamon
3 skeins

5975
rust
2 skeins

368
sand
5 skeins

374
beige
1 skein

352
dark brown
2 skeins

361
cream
2 skeins

341
coral
3 skeins

Canvas
14-gauge white interlock
Size: 38cm (15in) square

Other materials
Tapestry needle, size 20
Ruler or tape measure
Masking tape for binding the canvas
Sharp scissors for cutting the canvas
Embroidery scissors
Sharp HB pencil or fine permanent
  markers in suitable colours
Eraser

Marking the canvas
Cut the canvas to size and bind the edges with masking tape. This is a combined chart and artwork design. Trace the outline (from pages 148–9) on to the canvas with a permanent marker, using the straight outline as

a guide for the edge of the design. Follow the curved lines freely, ignoring the canvas grid. Trace the straight edge. When tracing straight lines use your discretion and mark the outline on the closest thread of the canvas.

If you are experienced it is not necessary to trace the fine lines, which are a guide to show where the colours on the tassels change. These fine lines can be disregarded or can be put on afterwards, freehand, in a different colour. A beginner may find it easier to follow the design by tracing the fine lines – do this with a permanent marker in a different colour, after you have finished tracing the thick lines.

Stitches used
TENT stitch (1) and reversed TENT stitch (1)
SATIN stitch (3)
STEM stitch (8)
For stitch instructions, see pages 144 and 145.

Stitching the tassels
The whole thread of the brown tapestry wool and six strands (the whole thread) of the stranded cotton have been used throughout this design.

The numbers on the coloured artwork refer to the stitch numbers. Look at the photograph of the made-up cushion and the coloured artwork to show you which colour goes

where. Work the tassels in diagonal SATIN stitch (3), STEM stitch (8) and TENT stitch (1). The cream 'crisscross' on the 'bobble' is worked in a combination of TENT stitch (1) and reversed TENT stitch (1).

Following the chart
When you have completed the stitching of the tassels, follow the colour chart above and 'fill in' the background. Remember that the squares of the chart represent the canvas intersections, not the holes. Each square represents one tent stitch.

The chart is divided up into units of 10 squares by 10 squares to make it easier to follow. Before beginning to stitch, it may be helpful to mark out your canvas in similar units of 10 squares by 10 squares with an HB pencil or permanent marker in a suitable colour.

The colours on the chart are shown stronger than the actual yarn colours to make them easier to see. The corresponding yarns are given in the colour key.

Stitching the background
The background in worked entirely in TENT stitch (1). Begin in any area you wish. It might be easiest to start by 'filling in' the stitches on either side of the tassels.

Making up instructions
When the design has been sewn, the needlepoint may need to be stetched back into shape (see stretching instructions on page 139). Then make it up into a cushion of your choice as shown on pages 140–1.

Fortuny. Ah, Fortuny. Called the magician of Venice, Renaissance man, genius, enigma . . . today he seems to us just as mysterious and fascinating. As well as a fabric designer, he saw himself as a painter, photographer, engraver, architect, inventor, set designer . . . he mixed art, craft and science with a creative fervour.

In his *palazzo* now, in the great studio-salon where he worked and entertained, we are drawn into an atmosphere of La Belle Epoque, the room hung with textiles and paintings like an exotic cave, with a sense of Fortuny having just gone out for a moment, wrapped in the cape he always wore. It is the fabrics that mesmerize us, the shimmering impressions of gold and silver, the amazing techniques he used to re-create the patinas found in metallic threads of antique materials. The sensuality of it all.

The end of the last century and the beginning of this saw a period of re-establishing the glorious style of the Middle Ages. Fortuny became inspired by fragments of ancient fabric found in Greece and, using his knowledge of antiquities and art as the basis for his research, began experimenting with various techniques, using artisans' almost-forgotten methods of dyeing and printing. He mixed techniques on a single length of fabric: brush, stencil, blocking, aluminium and bronze – on silk crêpe, taffeta, velvet and transparent gauzes – the results are still breathtakingly luxurious. He didn't copy old designs, but re-interpreted them – and his sources of inspiration went back to Crete and Mycenae and forward to eighteenth-century France, and much between: Coptic materials, geometrics and stripes from fragments at the Victoria and Albert Museum and the Louvre, minute florals from Persia and Turkey, motifs from Peru, Polynesia, Java, China, Japan and the Islamic world. He evoked the splendours of the Italian Renaissance, used the pomegranate and lotus of the fifteenth century, dipped into twelfth- and thirteenth-century Venetian brocades and borrowed from the religious paintings of Carpaccio and Bellini. He used designs from beautiful Venetian lace, and baroque and rococo floral velvets, wrought iron and architectural decoration. His fabrics perfectly imitated the ancient materials that so fascinated him, permeated with the patina of times long gone, using natural colours like indigo from India, cochineal from Mexico and herbal pigments from Brazil. His textiles are paintings and each is unique, the velvet, in particular, changing with the light. Proust described one of his pieces 'of an intense blue which, as my gaze extended over it, was changed into a malleable gold'.

Mariano Fortuny was born into a famous artistic Spanish family in Granada and his mother brought him to Venice in 1889, confident that in a city with no roads his allergy to horses would not be irritated. When he died in 1949, he left no children or grandchildren, his paintings and inventions were forgotten, only his exquisite fabrics endure as his legacy in a world of ephemera.

PURPLE BROCADE

This needlepoint was inspired by a fifteenth-century fabric in silk and metal thread in colours typical of that period – reminiscent, too, of Fortuny and La Belle Epoque. Work the design on 14 canvas for a beautiful cushion panel or, adding to and adapting the same chart, make a bolster, a floor cushion, what you will.

Finished size of design
18×28cm (7×11in)

Yarns
Anchor stranded cotton

☐ **830**
light beige
3 skeins

▨ **870**
lilac
4 skeins

▨ **871**
purple
2 skeins

▨ **392**
beige
1 skein

Appleton's tapestry wool
75cm (30in) lengths

▨ **607**
mauve
72 lengths

Astrella metallic thread

gold
2 skeins

Canvas
14-gauge white mono de luxe
Size: 28×38cm (11×15in)

Other materials
Tapestry needle, size 20
Ruler or tape measure
Masking tape for binding the canvas
Sharp scissors for cutting the canvas
Embroidery scissors
Sharp HB pencil or fine permanent
    marker in a suitable colour
Eraser

Following the chart
Cut the canvas to size and bind the edges with masking tape. The design does not have to be marked out on the canvas; just follow the colour chart on page 28. Remember that the squares represent the canvas intersections, not the holes. Each square represents one tent stitch.

The chart is divided up into units

of 10 squares by 10 squares to make it easier to follow. Before beginning to stitch, it may be helpful to mark out your canvas in similar units of 10 squares by 10 squares with an HB pencil or permanent marker in a suitable colour. Also, we suggest marking the top of the canvas so that if you turn it while stitching, you will still know where the top is.

The colours on the chart are shown stronger than the actual yarn colours. The corresponding yarns are given in the colour key.

Stitches used
TENT stitch (1) is used throughout. For stitch instructions, see page 144.

Stitching the design
Use six strands (the whole thread) of stranded cotton, the whole thread of gold thread and the whole thread of tapestry wool.

Begin in any area you wish. It might be easiest to start at the top right-hand corner, 4–5cm (1½–2in) in from the corner, working from one block of colour to another.

Making up instructions
When the design has been sewn, the needlepoint may need to be stretched back into shape (see stretching instructions on page 139). Then make it up into a cushion of your choice as shown on pages 140–1.

Yarns

Anchor stranded cotton

830
light beige
3 skeins

871
purple
2 skeins

870
lilac
4 skeins

392
beige
1 skein

Appleton's tapestry wool
75cm (30in) lengths

607
mauve
72 lengths

Astrella metallic thread

gold
2 skeins

You can traverse Venice top to bottom, side to side, in every quarter – you could even, as we have, eat your way round Venice *en route* to a particular waistcoat, a bodice, faded fragments laid to rest beneath glass like so many frayed butterflies. But it will be hard to imagine that you will see such glorious examples of work, so defiantly preserved and created with such dedication, as in the Ghetto in Venice. Among elaborate silver goblets, spice towers and scroll covers are stunning examples of embroidery.

Jews lived in Venice from the fourteenth century. They were useful to the city, they had financial acumen that endeared them to the Venetians and paid heavy taxes which endeared them even more. They were not dissimilar in temperament, even in looks, and were alike in that they both felt themselves 'set apart'. At a time in the early sixteenth century when Jews were being forcibly expelled from cities, Venice compromised in a way which was to become a model for many others to follow: it isolated the Jews in a closed quarter. The place chosen was a foundry – *getto* – and this gave its name to the first of the world's tragic ghettos. The Jews were compelled to live within its moat of canals and windowless outside walls, in houses which they had no choice but to develop upwards into Venetian 'skyscrapers' (they are still the tallest houses in Venice). There seven hundred Jews lived – the next century increasing to five thousand – and even flourished in the work permitted them: medicine, antiques, trading, money-lending. In the antique shops they could only sell used clothes, but as tailors and in the privacy of their own homes they created beautiful embroidered garments, worked on to fabric woven on hidden looms, and sold them with a 'second-hand' label sewn in.

The most staggering piece of embroidery in the Ghetto is a 'parochet', an immense curtain for the Holy Ark, with a very complex design showing the giving of the Commandments on Mount Sinai. It was made by Stella Perugia, who it seems must have been inspired by copies of Byzantine icons which she saw in Venice, possibly even by one particular icon, painted by one particular Domenikos Theotokopoulos, also known as El Greco. Young Domenikos settled in Venice at the time Titian and Tintoretto painted the walls of San Giorgio dei

Greci, and here he became dependent for his livelihood on the 'icon industry' much in demand on and around Rialto as religious souvenirs. The Sinai icon which was signed by El Greco (signing pictures was not usually accepted practice in those days) shows three mountaintops, as does Stella Perugia's parochet.

The parochet became the central feature of her life, perhaps of her entire community at that time. The inscription in the lower cartouche reads: 'made by the matron Stella Cohenet, wife of the magnificent esquire Yisrael of Perugia, the year 5394'. The year 5394 in the Hebrew calendar is 1634 . . . and the 'wife of the magnificent esquire'? Imagine receiving your mail addressed thus! As women, of course, we all understand the rumblings beneath the inscription, do we not? Let's hope that the magnificent esquire was appeased after years of coming home to his wife hunched over her embroidery, and the type of 'fish by fire, slippers in oven' instructions so familiar to husbands of needle-obsessed wives. 'Stella loves her little hobby,' he probably said to his friends, thinking, 'This is a bit big for a tray cloth. Why doesn't she do keep fit, or calligraphy, like the other wives?'

The key to unravelling (an unfortunate phrase, strike it from the records), the key to interpreting the parochet is Psalm 36 – the design is full of biblical symbolism. In recent years the Venetian/Israeli artist David Pe'er, while producing a modern print of the parochet, noticed the numerology involved in the embroidery. God is one, the tablets are two, Mount Sinai's peaks, as in the icons, three, there are four ships on the sea, six towers on the City of David. He says there is no symbol for five, but there do seem to be five inscriptions on the walls of Jerusalem . . .

After her death in 1673, Stella Perugia's headstone in the Lido cemetery was engraved:

> *Such an innocent and sincere woman,*
> *Radiating light on her path,*
> *And with great wisdom embroidered tapestry,*
> *She made a parochet and completed it in days of purity*
> *and in sanctity, toiling mightily, alone . . .*

This story was told to us by a lady in the Ghetto, a descendant of Sara Copio Sullman, a poetess who held a famous literary salon in the Ghetto attended by Venetian aristocrats and intellectuals of the seventeenth century.

Left: A section of the 'parochet', a curtain for the Holy Ark in the Ghetto, showing the floral motifs we have used overleaf in the oval picture. The design is worked on canvas in crewel wool and pearl cotton, repeating the diamond shapes seen on the original. Photographed at Rina Zennaro's treasure-chest of a shop (see page 129), a place to hold your breath lest generations of objets are disturbed.

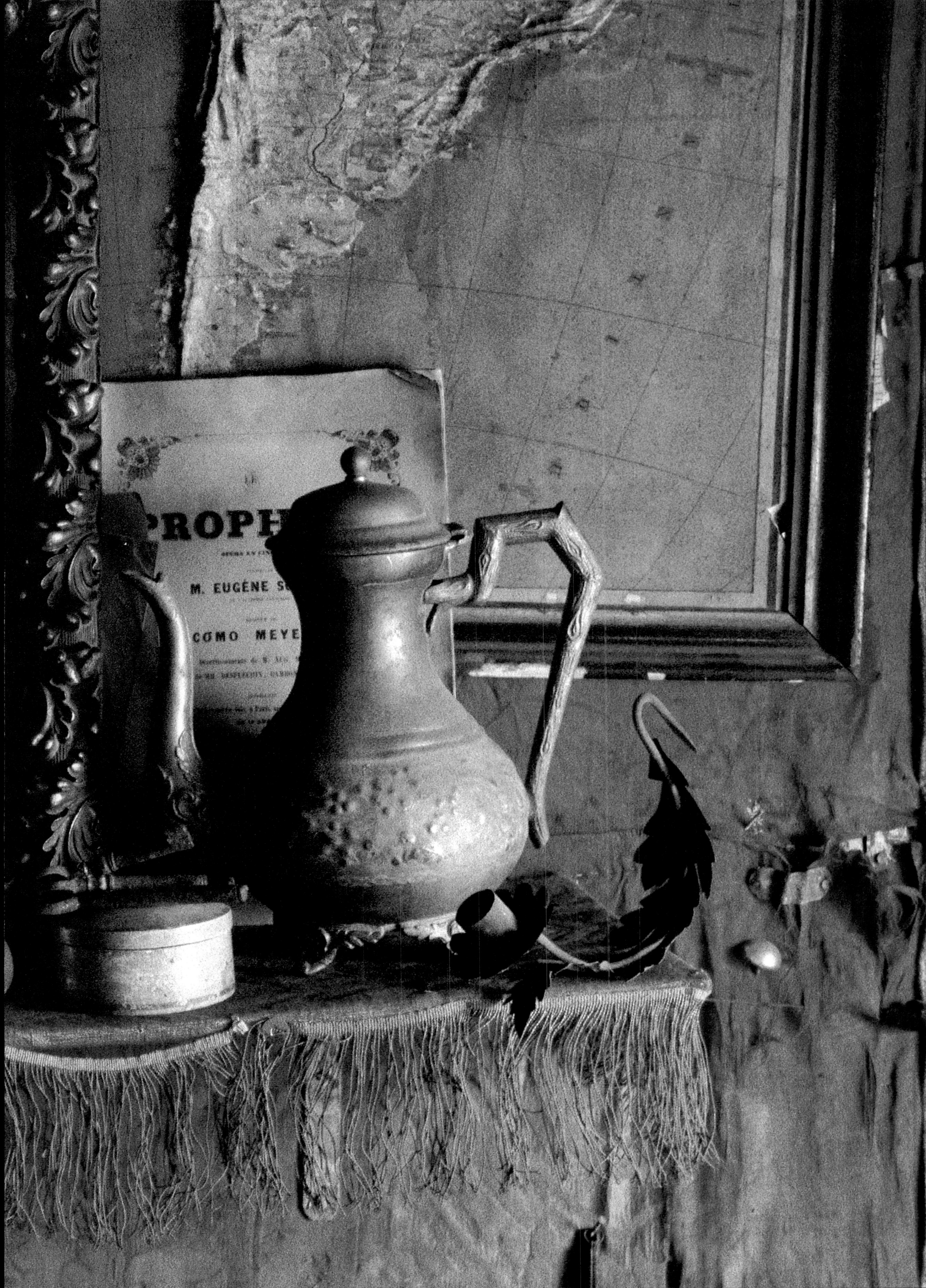
PROPH
M. EUGÈNE S
COMO MEYE

PAROCHET FRAGMENT

The design was taken from a section of an exquisite embroidered curtain for the Holy Ark from the Venice Ghetto, probably worked in the seventeenth century. It depicts dramatic bouquets on a trellis, which can be worked in stitchery or in tent stitch throughout.

Finished size of design
14×18cm (5½×7in)

Yarns
Appleton's crewel wool

851 yellow 1 skein	**932** mauve 1 skein
901 ochre 1 skein	**741** blue 1 skein
621 peach 1 skein	**341** pale green 2 skeins
221 bois de rose 1 skein	**293** green 1 skein
223 crimson 1 skein	

DMC coton perlé No.5

ecru
2 skeins

Canvas
18-gauge white interlock
Size: 24×28cm (9½×11in)

Other materials
Tapestry needle, size 22
Ruler or tape measure
Masking tape for binding the canvas
Sharp scissors for cutting the canvas
Embroidery scissors
Sharp HB pencil or fine permanent
  marker in a suitable colour
Eraser
Tracing paper and fine black marker

Method 1: Using tent stitch

Following the chart
Cut the canvas to size and bind the

edges with masking tape. The design does not have to be marked out on the canvas; just follow the colour chart opposite. Remember that the squares represent the canvas inter-sections, not the holes. Each square represents one tent stitch.

The chart is divided up into units of 10 squares by 10 squares to make it easier to follow. Before beginning to stitch, it may be helpful to mark out your canvas in similar units of 10 squares by 10 squares with an HB pencil or permanent marker in a suitable colour. Also, we suggest marking the top of the canvas so that if you turn it while stitching, you will still know where the top is.

The colours on the chart are shown stronger than the actual yarn colours to make them easier to see. The corresponding yarns are given in the colour key.

Stitches used
TENT stitch (1) is used throughout. For stitch instructions, see page 144.

Stitching the design
Two strands of crewel wool are used throughout, and the whole thread of coton perlé. Begin in any area you wish; it might be easiest to start in the top right-hand corner, 4–5cm (1½–2in) in from the corner, working from one block of colour to another.

Method 2: Using stitchery

Marking the canvas
Cut the canvas to size and bind the edges with masking tape. Trace the floral design including the oval outline (from page 157) on to the canvas with a permanent marker, centring the tracing. Follow the curved lines freely, ignoring the canvas grid. When tracing straight lines, use your discretion and mark the outline on the closest thread of the canvas. The red outlines on the trace pattern denote which of the flowers have stitchery, the black outlines denote which flowers are in TENT stitch (1).

Stitches used
TENT stitch (1)
SATIN stitch (3)
LONG AND SHORT stitch (7)
For stitch instructions, see pages 144 and 145.

Stitching the design and following the chart
Two strands of crewel wool are used throughout and the whole thread of coton perlé.

The numbers on the tracing refer to the stitch numbers. Look at the photograph of the made-up picture and at the colour chart to show you which colour goes where. The flowers have been stitched in SATIN stitch (3),

LONG AND SHORT stitch (7) and TENT stitch (1).

When you have sewn the flowers, follow the colour chart for the background, which is worked in TENT stitch (1). Begin in any area you wish; it may be easiest to start from the edge of the flowers on a trellis line and fill in as you go along.

Making up instructions
When the design has been sewn, the needlepoint may need to be stretched back into shape (see stretching instructions on page 139). You may prefer to take your needlepoint to a professional picture framer who will also stretch it for you.

DECORATIVE VENICE

DECORATIVE VENICE

In Piazza di San Marco where, in the days of the Republic, bullfights and bearbaitings, executions and ceremonies of state took place, and where the legacy of the square as marketplace is still mapped out on the inlaid pavement lines, the echoes are there if we listen in the early morning, as the first shopkeepers open up, and the man we call the defrocked priest delivers his daily sermon to the pigeons and blesses any early passers-by.

Visits to other cathedrals are no preparation for the Basilica di San Marco. Charles Dickens described it thus:

> *I thought I entered a Cathedral, and went in and out among its many arches: traversing its whole extent. A grand and dreamy structure, of immense proportions; golden with old mosaics; redolent of perfumes; dim with the smoke of incense; costly in treasure of precious stones and metals, glittering through iron bars; holy with the bodies of deceased saints; rainbow-hued with windows of stained glass; dark with carved woods and coloured marbles; obscure in its vast heights and lengthened distances, shining with silver lamps and winking lights; unreal, fantastic, solemn, inconceivable throughout.*

There are various explanations for the dark purple smell in the Basilica – be it incense, animal fat rubbed into the marble to achieve its gleam, an army of wet raincoats and ubiquitous sneakers, candle wax and smoke; all interlace their webs to create an atmosphere that weights the air almost tangibly.

The building is extraordinary, from the top of the onion domes to the glorious multiple hues of the marble columns, the porphyries, serpentines, jaspers, the Carraras, some at least with the pretence of holding up the frontage, others just standing like token guests at the wedding ('Alfredo! Haven't got enough porphyry-red along this side. Put a couple more pillars at that end!'). The wall mosaics here and on the island of Torcello are justifiably famous, but it is the floors that interest us more. Before thinking 'needlepoint', we had walked over the mosaics with only superficial appreciation. Now a floodgate of patterning opened up. Did you ever lie in bed as a child and make pictures from the woodchip paper on the ceiling? Marble becomes like that. When hungry, we can see in the veining liquorice allsorts and mottled slabs of sliced salami scattered with squares of fat. After a prolonged lunch the imagination is a little more fuelled and it is quite easy to see cities in microcosm, aeons of mineral layers in abstract whirlpools.

There seems surprisingly little documentation about the floors and, as the Basilica shopkeeper trembles on the verge of breakdown at the request for more information, we take copious photographs. As we crouch low for detail, tourists give a wide berth, assuming a contact lens has been dropped. It is very dark on the Basilica floor and by rights the stone should be quite dull. It is not. The gloriously interlocked little shapes glow with a thousand tones, their imperfect angles and cracks picking up whatever glow comes from walls and candles. There are great satisfying blocks of disciplined pattern, veering off into tramlines and railway tracks and then circling cross-sections that look like bone marrow and Fair-Isle sweaters, and some are so ingenious that only computer graphics could compete, others so naïve that they are reminiscent of a child with gummed paper shapes. It seems they evolved with their own impetus, marching from the high altar out to the square in great undulations, making the floor a living kaleidoscope in pink, slate, emerald, ochre and terracotta shimmers. Only by looking closely do the riches become obvious, and the needle hand itches to try that combination: wild and controlled at the same time.

* * *

At the time of writing, the Lion of Venice sits in greater comfort than usual (though with a less spectacular view) in the British Museum, not on his usual vertiginous column top in the Piazzetta, scorched in summer, shrouded in winter. The lion is one of the four winged biblical beasts and in early Christian art became the symbol of St Mark the Evangelist. Legend has it that while St Mark was travelling from Aquileia to Rome, his ship docked at Venice, where a timely angel said 'Peace to you, Mark, here shall rest your body' – and how many of us have heard that same angel?

The origins of the huge bronze Lion are unclear. Archaeologists and art historians are agreed that it came from Iran in the sixth century, Venice in the thirteenth century, was a cult statue made in the Near East about 300 BC and also came from China. The surviving, unrestored pieces of lion suggest that he was winged, possibly even horned. In 1797 he was carried off to Paris, and after Napoleon's fall the decision was made to return him. The French had a small accident, possibly in baggage handling, which resulted in major restoration, much as we see him today: from a distance looking up from the Piazzetta, magnificent and dignified; from close up, a hideous hybrid from Hammer films.

With today's technology, we forget the difficulties of dragging a massive bronze lion up and down its column – even of transporting and erecting the Piazzetta's granite columns themselves. The successful engineer who achieved this feat was promised the gambling monopoly of Venice, provided the sessions were held between these two columns. Unfortunately for the hero, this was also the site of the scaffold for public executions. The Casino is now in Ca' Vendramin Calergi, and, at 3 o'clock on a filthy winter afternoon, is probably the only place in Venice where you'll see a queue waiting for the doors to open. In the summer the Casino has a home on the Lido – there are wonderful old memories of parents and their friends, after not even very spectacular wins, with pockets bulging and overflowing with lire. In those days particularly, lire looked like so much money!

Back to the Lion. He sits, poor glued-together composite, alongside the Doge's Palace. If Rome calls her Victor Emmanuel Monument the 'Wedding Cake', what does that make this gorgeous pink-iced filigree Palace? It sits comfortably as it has since the fourteenth century, balanced on its baseless columns. The carvings on the capitals are much restored, but they are charming, and particularly touching is the one showing court-ship, the first kiss, marriage, birth of the child, death of the child (seventh column into the Piazzetta from the sea).

No one seems clear what makes the Palace pink, though its façade was certainly designed for needlepoint. The architect has imitated the mixing of crewel wools so cleverly in stone, matching to the Appleton's shade card, for which we thank him. We have used the design for the stool overleaf, and it will adapt to any size – from the daintiest work on 18 canvas to a slip cover for a palace, probably worked on 5-gauge canvas, which is how the Venetians have used it.

Opposite: The interior of the Basilica di San Marco, painted by Albert Goodwin, which conveys to us the heaviness of the incense-laden atmosphere.
Above: The ubiquitous Venetian pigeons, strutting against the elaborate pink façade of the Doge's Palace. Our stool top project overleaf imitates the interlocking colours of the shaded marble – coral, terracotta, stone and grey.

DOGE'S BARGELLO STOOL

This stool top was inspired by the exquisite interlocked stonework of the façade of the Doge's Palace. The strands of crewel wool are mixed to emulate the gradations of coral tones, and the centre of each pattern is randomly coloured as in the Palace itself.

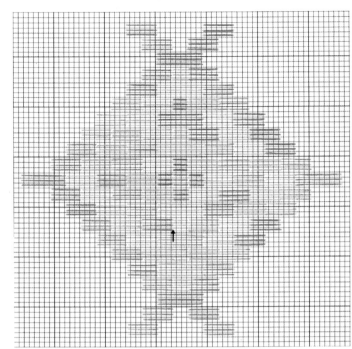

Finished size of design
38cm (15in) square

Yarns
Appleton's crewel wool

151 blue 2 skeins		**203** pale coral 8 skeins	
881 cream 10 skeins		**204** dark coral 8 skeins	
988 beige 7 skeins			

Canvas
16-gauge white mono de luxe
Size: 48cm (19in) square

Other materials
Tapestry needle, size 22
Ruler or tape measure
Masking tape for binding the canvas
Sharp scissors for cutting the canvas
Embroidery scissors
Sharp HB pencil or fine permanent
   marker in a suitable colour
Eraser

Marking the canvas
Draw a 38cm (15in) square on the thread of the canvas, using an HB pencil or permanent marker. Find the centre point by drawing a diagonal from one corner to the other (see *figs. 1* and *2*), following either the 'under' or the 'over' threads of the canvas consistently. Mark the centre of the canvas with a small cross.

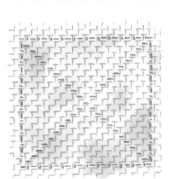

fig. 1

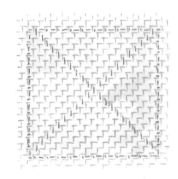

fig. 2

Stitches used
Horizontal SATIN stitch (3) is used throughout, worked over three, six and nine threads of the canvas. For stitch instructions, see page 144.

Stitching the design
Three strands of crewel wool have been used. For the areas towards the centre cut your thread to approximately 30cm (12in) in length. As you

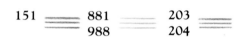

151	881	203
	988	204

progress it does not have to be so short to give a random effect. You can use lengths of 38–46cm (15–18in).

Follow the chart above and the photograph of the made-up stool. First thread the needle with one strand of 988 and two of 881 and work the area around the central inner cross, following the chart (fill in all the inner crosses at the end). Begin at the arrow and then, when the wool has run out, thread the needle randomly, first with two strands of 988 and one strand of 881; then three strands of 988 and finally three strands of 881. Do the same for the coral wool; two strands of 204 and one of 203; two of 203 and one of 204; three of 203; three of 204. The idea is to sew randomly to give this design a faded look.

Complete the creamy stone areas and the coral areas. Finally put in the inner crosses using three strands of blue wool 151, and the centre squares in cream or coral.

Making up instructions
When the design has been sewn, the needlepoint may need to be stretched back into shape (see stretching instructions on page 139). Then make it up into a square stool or, alternatively, a cushion of your choice (as shown on pages 140–1).

MOSAIC

Design elements are taken from the mosaic floors of the Basilica di San Marco, glorious interlocked shapes of porphyry, serpentine and jasper in dozens of shades from pink to peacock.

Finished size of design
33cm (13in) square

Yarns
Appleton's tapestry wool
75cm (30in) lengths

881 stone 60 lengths	**153** mid turquoise 18 lengths
202 mushroom 21 lengths	**155** dark turquoise 18 lengths
478 burnt orange 18 lengths	**157** bottle green 45 lengths
765 ginger 18 lengths	**184** brown 9 lengths
761 honey 24 lengths	**182** beige 81 lengths
151 pale turquoise 36 lengths	**293** Jacobean green 12 lengths
876 ice blue 54 lengths	

Canvas
14-gauge white mono de luxe
Size: 43cm (17in) square

Other materials
Tapestry needle, size 20
Masking tape for binding the canvas
Sharp scissors for cutting the canvas
Embroidery scissors
Sharp HB pencil or fine permanent
   marker in a suitable colour
Eraser

Following the chart
Cut the canvas to size and bind the edges with masking tape. The design

does not have to be marked out on the canvas; just follow the colour chart on page 42. Remember that the squares represent the canvas intersections, not the holes. Each square represents one tent stitch.

The chart is divided up into units of 10 squares by 10 squares to make it easier to follow. Before beginning to stitch, it may be helpful to mark out your canvas in similar units of 10 squares by 10 squares with an HB pencil or permanent marker in a suitable colour. Also, we suggest marking the top of the canvas so that if you turn the canvas while stitching, you will still know where the top is.

The colours on the chart are shown stronger than the actual yarn

colours to make them easier to see. The corresponding yarns are given in the colour key.

Stitches used
TENT stitch (1) and ▣ reversed TENT stitch (1) are used throughout this design. For stitch instructions, see page 144.

Stitching the design
Use the whole thread of tapestry wool throughout.

Begin in any area you wish. It might be easiest to start at the top right-hand corner, 4–5cm (1½–2in) in from the corner, working from one block of colour to another.

The symbols on the chart show the areas of reversed tent stitch.

Yarns

Appleton's tapestry wool
75cm (30in) lengths

881
stone
60 lengths

202
mushroom
21 lengths

478
burnt orange
18 lengths

765
ginger
18 lengths

761
honey
24 lengths

151
pale turquoise
36 lengths

876
ice blue
54 lengths

153
mid turquoise
18 lengths

155
dark turquoise
18 lengths

157
bottle green
45 lengths

184
brown
9 lengths

182
beige
81 lengths

293
Jacobean green
12 lengths

Making up instructions

When the design has been sewn, the needlepoint may need to be stretched back into shape (see stretching instructions on page 139). Then make it up into a cushion of your choice as shown on pages 140–1.

Opposite: Chair seat worked on 7-gauge canvas, using a mixture of motifs from the Mosaic cushion design and a little improvisation! The pattern can be adapted to many sizes and purposes.

Opposite the Basilica in the Piazza, under the great grey colonnades (with their blinds festooned in cold folds that sometimes appear marble and at other times look as languorous as Southern belles), there, where the wind always seems to hover, are two sets of wrought-iron gates and a flight of marble stairs that will take you to the Correr.

The Correr Museum is housed in Napoleon's own wing of the Procuratie Nuove – a space was left for him in the centre of the sculpted Roman emperors on the roof, but no one ever put him there. Teodoro Correr gave his collection to Venice in 1830. Henry James called it 'a thousand curious mementoes and relics', and Mrs Correr was probably pleased to get it out of the house. It makes us think of Lady John Soane, in her house in London's Lincoln's Inn. There are portraits of her there and she is definitely Not Happy (and indeed who would be, with a collection of bizarre antiquities large enough to fill an aeroplane hangar squeezed into her back parlour?). It isn't difficult to imagine another sarcophagus being tiptoed past the ladies at her Monday bridge evening: 'I SAW THAT, JOHN, don't think I didn't! Where do you expect me to put all this STUFF?' Poor Lady Soane, she may well have sympathized with Mrs Correr.

For those interested in such things, the Museum is splendid and contains robes, documents, arms, coins and maps that chart Venice's history. For those interested in beauty, not war, go to the second floor to see the two extraordinary inlaid tables from which we took the Correr project opposite. The tables are large, made of thick stone with elaborate and exquisite intarsia of flora and fauna: birds, butterflies, little creatures, buds and fruits bursting, in a hundred colours of stone and mineral, all done with imagination and wit too rarely seen.

We have made the cushion octagonal – it could also be made square – and have left the background uncoloured on the painted artwork on page 47, so that the effect of changing the charcoal for a paler background can be seen. The vase on the original is a true lapis lazuli blue and the flowers multicoloured slivers of agates, marbles and minerals. Deciding what to leave out was almost a sacrilege. To do justice to the concept of such a design in needlepoint, it needed to be, at least, a carpet for a ballroom – if not a football pitch. However, what we have is a cushion, which can be worked in fast-flowing long and short stitch for the flowers and leaves and more structured and disciplined stitches for the vase and scrolls. We didn't want to imitate the stone with this needlepoint, simply to translate an unyielding surface into a warm textile; where we have been faithful is in the vibrancy of colour. We have the texture of stitch instead of the veining of stone, and the flowers still glow like jewels.

Above: The section of the magnificent stone table in the Correr Museum that inspired our octagonal cushion opposite – glorious spring flowers on a charcoal background contained within scrolls, originally inlaid with stone, now embossed with wool.

CORRER

The design for the octagonal cushion comes from an inlaid table in the Correr Museum — the inlay is in stone and minerals, a glorious multi-coloured celebration of flora and fauna. The section we have chosen shows a lapis lazuli vase and brilliant spring flowers within a scrolled border.

Finished size of design
33cm (13in) square

Yarn
Anchor tapisserie wool

386 cream 3 skeins		**721** pale olive 2 skeins	
729 pale yellow 2 skeins		**3045** beige 2 skeins	
3229 mid yellow 2 skeins		**843** dark olive 2 skeins	
3000 dark yellow 3 skeins		**139** blue 2 skeins	
368 apricot 1 skein		**403** charcoal 15 skeins	
427 orange 3 skeins			

Canvas
14-gauge white interlock
Size: 41cm (16in) square

Other materials
Tapestry needle, size 20
Ruler or tape measure
Masking tape for binding the canvas
Sharp scissors for cutting the canvas
Embroidery scissors
Sharp HB pencil or fine permanent
   markers in suitable colours
Eraser
Tracing paper and fine black marker
Adhesive tape

Marking the canvas
Cut the canvas to size and bind the edges with masking tape. Starting about 4cm (1½in) vertically and

horizontally from the top right-hand corner, draw a 33cm (13in) square on the thread of the canvas. Count 30 holes in horizontally from the top right-hand corner of the square and mark the spot. Likewise count down 30 holes vertically and mark the spot. Draw a diagonal line on the thread of the canvas from A to B. Repeat this on all four corners. This outline marks the finished shape of the octagonal cushion.

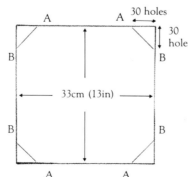

As you will see, only half of the border is outlined on page 151. Take two tracings of the border with tracing paper and a black marker. Reverse one and join them with adhesive tape. Position the border under the canvas, using the outline as a guide, and trace the border using a permanent marker. Follow the curved lines freely, ignoring the canvas grid. When tracing straight lines, use your discretion and mark the outline on the closest thread.

Trace the outline of the vase of flowers from pages 150–1, centring the design within the border. If you are experienced, it is not necessary to trace the fine lines, which are a guide to show where the colours on the flowers and leaves change. These fine lines can be disregarded or can be put on afterwards, freehand, in a different colour. A beginner may

need to trace the fine lines – do this in a different colour, after you have traced the thick lines.

Stitches used
TENT stitch (1)
CHAIN stitch (2)
SATIN stitch (3)
LONG AND SHORT stitch (7)
STEM stitch (8)
BRICK stitch over two threads (12)
For stitch instructions, see pages 144, 145 and 147.

Stitching the design
The whole thread is used throughout.

The numbers on the artwork refer to the stitch numbers. For the position and direction of the stitches and to see which colour yarn goes where, refer to the photograph of the made-up cushion and the coloured artwork. The arrows show the stitch direction. Remember that this is a guide; don't be restricted by it, and feel free to experiment.

The flowers are worked in LONG AND SHORT stitch (7), some TENT stitch (1), STEM stitch (8) and SATIN stitch (3) where indicated. CHAIN stitch (2) has been used for the stems. Horizontal and vertical BRICK stitch (12) over two threads has been used for the leaves.

The butterflies are worked in LONG AND SHORT stitch (7) with

diagonal SATIN stitch (3) on the body. The antennae are in STEM stitch (8). The vase is sewn in vertical BRICK stitch (12) over two threads with STEM stitch (8).

The border is worked in SATIN stitch (3) edged in STEM stitch (8). The background is sewn in TENT stitch (1) worked as basketweave, in charcoal or to your choice.

Making up instructions
When the design has been sewn, the needlepoint may need to be stretched back into shape (see stretching instructions on page 139). Then make it up into a cushion of your choice as shown on pages 140–1.

Many Venetian walls have exquisite plaster decorations, usually great swirling leaves and blooms embossed in white plaster on pastel backgrounds stretching from floor to ceiling. A needlepoint project from them would not be interesting to work, but we have sneaked in some similar panels on the outside of the Shells cushion on page 80 and some leaves on the Carnival cushion on page 110. There are particularly beautiful examples on pistachio green backgrounds in Ca' Querini Stampalia, a tiny museum near Campo Santa Maria Formosa. The ground floor has been modernized to create the atmosphere of a Zen garden, quite a surprise for Venice, where planning restrictions usually seem more in force than in some cities, where the rule seems to be the nastier the better. There is a library, and more atmospheric paintings of Venetian life by Longhi, as well as beautiful pieces (and we mean pieces) of textiles and tapestry, tassels and braids.

* * *

The Curtain Tie-back opposite was inspired by carved stone-work that we first saw around a door at the Frari (Santa Maria Gloriosa Dei Frari, or Ca' Grande for short). It is a decoration that is repeated on other churches – San Stefano has similar barley-sugar scrolls, alternate rows of spirals and heavily carved leaves in dramatic bands of stone. The design would adapt wonderfully to other shapes and sizes, and to tones of colours other than grey, and the scrolls

would be perfect for borders. If you are ever in Venice and near the Frari, do look at these beautiful carvings, and while there, go straight to the high altar in that great dim place and pay open-mouthed homage to Titian's *Assumption* (anything less is inappropriate) and think what a needlepoint project that would make!

Above: Columns outside the Basilica, and examples of the decorative effects the city offers at every turn.
Opposite: The Curtain Tie-back inspired by stone carvings at the entrance to the Church of the Frari.

FRARI CURTAIN TIE-BACK

Inspired by the dramatic carved stonework around the entrance to the Church of the Frari, barley-sugar scrolls surround a band of heavily elaborate leaves. Separate elements of the design could adapt excellently to different sizes and colours for beautiful borders.

Yarns
Appleton's tapestry wool
75cm (30in) lengths

883 heather 66 lengths

933 plum 27 lengths

962 pale grey 63 lengths

141 mushroom 24 lengths

964 dark grey 90 lengths

DMC coton perlé No.3

white 3 skeins

Finished size of design
66×15cm (26×6in) approximately

Canvas
14-gauge white mono de luxe
Size: 76×26cm (30×10in)

Other materials
Tapestry needle, size 20
Ruler or tape measure
Masking tape for binding the canvas
Sharp scissors for cutting the canvas
Embroidery scissors
Sharp HB pencil or fine permanent
   marker in a suitable colour
Eraser

Following the chart
Cut the canvas to size and bind the edges with masking tape. The design does not have to be marked out on the canvas; just follow the colour chart below. Remember that the squares represent the canvas inter-sections, not the holes. Each square represents one tent stitch.

The chart is divided up into units of 10 squares by 10 squares to make it easier to follow. Before beginning to stitch, it may be helpful to mark out your canvas in similar units of 10 squares by 10 squares with an HB pencil or permanent marker in a suitable colour. Also, we suggest marking the top of the canvas so that if you turn the canvas while you are stitching, you will still know where the top is.

The colours on the chart are shown stronger than the actual yarn colours to make them easier to see. The corresponding yarns are given in the colour key.

Stitches used
TENT stitch (1) is used throughout this project. For stitch instructions, see page 144.

Stitching the design
Use the whole thread of tapestry wool and also the whole thread of coton perlé.

Begin in any area you wish. It might be easiest to start at the top right-hand corner, 4–5cm (1½–2in) in from the corner, working from one block of colour to another.

Making up instructions
When the design has been sewn, the needlepoint may need to be stretched back into shape (see stretching instructions on page 139). Then make it up into a tie-back as shown on page 142.

Externally, Ca' Rezzonico is one of the least attractive *palazzi* on the Grand Canal, looming like a threatening mausoleum. In 1935 it was sold to the municipality, who filled it with furniture and paintings from the Correr Museum. Internally, Ca' Rezzonico is for fantasizing what life was like (for a few) in eighteenth-century Venice. Ignore the boring bits that only we fanatics find riveting – the draped walls, the shredded brocade – and go to the third floor for the puppets and apothecary shop and work your way down for wonderful Tiepolo frescoes and Longhi paintings, gorgeous little boy cherubs, possibly the most ridiculous furniture in Venice and glorious views from the windows.

The nicest way to arrive at Ca' Rezzonico is from San Samuele by *traghetto* – the gondolas that go from one side of the canal to the other (the locals stand, but don't try this after a heavy lunch). Browning called the palace 'a corner for my old age' and did in fact die here, and the municipality inscribed a plaque that reads:

> Open my heart and you will see
> Graved inside of it 'Italy'.

Browning never owned Ca' Rezzonico, although it is generally thought that he did. Much to his delight, in 1887 his son, who had married an American heiress, bought the palace. Browning Jnr restored Ca' Rezzonico magnificently, but it was only two years later that the inclemency of the Venetian weather proved too much for Robert Browning's health, and he died. A little later the heiress left, unable to tolerate her husband or his 'stately temple to the rococo' any longer.

The design which we have used for the stool top shown here and overleaf came from a lacquered door painted with Chinese figures and beribboned bouquets, made in Venice around 1750, absolutely beautiful and framed senselessly by damask curtains and a gilt pelmet. We have simplified, but kept as closely as we can to the warm colours and feeling of the original.

The Ca' Rezzonico stool photographed in Contessa Maria Franchin's palazzo, with three formally dressed chairs. The Contessa wanted to undress the chairs – no, we said, keep their frocks on.

CA' REZZONICO STOOL

Ca' Rezzonico is the palace where Robert Browning lived and died, and this floral stool was inspired by a lacquered door there, painted with Chinese figures and beribboned bouquets. The same design is shown on an octagonal stool and a round stool, and could be adapted to make a beautiful central motif on a square cushion or seat.

Finished size of design
Circle 29cm (11½in) in diameter or a 29cm (11½in) square

Yarns
Appleton's tapestry wool
75cm (30in) lengths

877
peach
132 lengths

143
plum
21 lengths

621
pale flamingo
9 lengths

693
pale ochre
27 lengths

623
flamingo
18 lengths

475
dark ochre
18 lengths

541
light green
21 lengths

841
lemon
9 lengths

643
dark green
30 lengths

Canvas
14-gauge white mono interlock
Size: 40cm (15½in) square

Other materials
Tapestry needle, size 20
Ruler or tape measure
Masking tape for binding the canvas
Sharp scissors for cutting the canvas
Embroidery scissors

Sharp HB pencil or fine permanent markers in suitable colours
Eraser
Pair of compasses

Marking the canvas
Cut the canvas to size and bind the edges with masking tape. If you decide to make this design circular, draw a circle 29cm (11½in) in diameter on to the centre of the canvas with the pair of compasses. If you make it square, you will need more background wool.

Trace the outline (from pages 152–3) on to the canvas with a pencil or permanent marker, centring the tracing. Follow the curved lines

freely, ignoring the canvas grid.

If you are experienced it is not necessary to trace the fine lines, which are a guide to show where the colours on the flowers and leaves change. These fine lines can be disregarded or can be put on afterwards, freehand, in a different colour. A beginner may need to trace the fine lines – do this in a different colour, after you have traced the thick lines.

Stitches used
TENT stitch (1)
SATIN stitch (3)
FRENCH KNOTS (5)
LONG AND SHORT stitch (7)
STEM stitch (8)

For stitch instructions, see pages 144 and 145.

Stitching the design
Use the whole thread of tapestry wool throughout. The numbers on the coloured artwork refer to the stitch numbers. Refer to the photograph of the made-up stool and the coloured artwork to show you which colour goes where. Remember that this is a guide; do feel free to experiment.

Begin by working the flowers in LONG AND SHORT stitch (7) and

TENT stitch (1). The buds are in SATIN stitch (3). The centres of the flowers have been worked in FRENCH KNOTS (5). The leaves have been sewn using TENT stitch (1) and SATIN stitch (3). The stems are in STEM stitch (8). The border is in vertical and horizontal SATIN stitch (3) – vertical at the top and bottom, horizontal at the two sides – edged in STEM stitch (8). Finally fill in the background in TENT stitch (1).

Making up instructions
When the design has been sewn, the needlepoint may need to be stretched back into shape (see stretching instructions on page 139). Then make it up into a stool as on page 142.

UFFICI

BACKSTREETS AND

BACKWATERS

Venice must be the world's most photogenic city. It can arrange reflections, mists, peach marble sunrises, baroque, Gothic, cherubic, theatrical façades with upturned profiles at the drop of a lens hood. It is a Cecil B. De Mille production of a city, the extras are brought in by the coachload, the rotting garbage powdered with saccharine, the closing soundtrack the predictable distanced solitary footsteps.

A less popular form of photography happens for a book. How many people do you see manoeuvring lights and tripods through alleyways? The light carrier leads the procession. He knows the way, yes. This way? Oh. He is followed by the cushion carrier, the photographer and bearer of cameras, a flower child shielding a perfect stem of mimosa, a piece of furniture, designer black bin liners.

Ca' Corner-Spinelli – the first house in Venice to be influenced by Renaissance design – is now home to Rubelli fabrics and yielded beautiful painted doors and backdrops

and a view of the Grand Canal that Henry James described as: 'with its immense field of confused reflection . . . the dullest expanse in Venice'. Indeed, we all yawned, how boring. Not another exquisite view. The entrance hall was sombre and dark, with great stone benches, marbled. A serious entrance hall, we said. The stone benches were the icy length of an exhausted body and we lay morguishly a while, futilely waiting for energy to return. Venice may make the heart flutter, the mind reel – it also makes the feet, calves, knees and back ache.

Geraniums in window boxes. Dull turquoise and bottle green shutters, fragments of lace curtains, as much part of Venice as the canal fragrance, and a picture irresistible for needlepoint. You know by the flutter of lace that the room inside will be dark, there will be heavy polished wood, antimacassars and a rosebowl of artificial flowers. The Geraniums picture overleaf was photographed in Castello – keep walking *sempre diritto* from San Marco along the Riva degli Schiavoni. Everything, so the saying goes, is *sempre diritto* in Venice – straight

ahead – although little actually is and the instruction will be accompanied by much snaking of the wrist.

The Geraniums picture was positioned in front of the stunning red-and-green wall. The sun swept its winter way into the *calle*, and as the shadows shrank and flooded light across wall and needlepoint, an upstairs window opened and the signora sent out her clothes-line of wet troops, as if to protect the modesty of the street. The shadow of candlewick bathmat fell across the picture. She refused to move it, nor did begging and bribing help. These things are wet, she said, not understanding such stupidity. Ian, who with his brilliant persuasive Italian helped us photograph where angels feared to tread, was not there. Ian was charming Florian's into agreeing to a morning's photographic disruption. Ian, it was agreed, could charm birds off trees, and certainly candlewick bathmats off lines.

Authors' historic photographic note: There are plaques on wall and pavement just at the end of the Merceria where it joins Piazza di San Marco, dedicated to Giustina Rossi, a lady who accidentally knocked a piece of cement from her window sill as she watched an uprising in 1311. It fell on the head of the standard bearer, was seen as an omen and she became a heroine. However, new research has brought to light that history was wrong. Giustina Rossi was in fact on a photographic shoot and craning out of her window to check the exact moment the morning sun entered the archway from the square, under the bell tower.

* * *

At first the backstreets seem very similar, then subtle differences register on the hypnotized eye to give us clues around the maze . . . a particular hardware shop, a more elaborate well than the others, a wall conspiratorially leaning across the *calle*, a tabernacle with water in the plastic flower vases. The maze zigzags, a sharp turn, a tiny overhung walkway, a corner building narrowing to a gingerbread house sliver, and then curving on to a slab of Gothic *palazzo* wall. The plaster skin flakes to reveal the brick bones of the walls, and among the uniform peelings are polished brass name plates: doctor, lawyer. Unexpectedly, from the apex of a little bridge, you may see an astonishing frescoed ceiling, elaborate plaster decorations, a ludicrous chandelier.

Venice is washing. While the bricks of Venice close its outside face, they also reveal the stuff of life in a wonderfully basic way. In Castello, where the *calli* are wider, the colours Rothko, the graffiti Jackson Pollock, the washing is scenery – the school of Venetian Expressionism. A designer could never contrive turquoise and kingfisher shirts to echo the shades of the shutters with such success, or create shrines to the victims of war with such touching charm – a madonna draped with pearls, the simplicity of the candles. Tiny courtyards with their rain-collecting wells, carved niches; carved riches. The Italians think in stone, the light reflects on it, no earth to absorb and bake. Water and stone, the sea yields its treasures, the stone yields to the sea.

* * *

Round Venetian windows, in shades of amethyst and topaz, distorting the city outside. Occasionally, an old circle may be replaced with clear glass and, like a keyhole, brings a fragment of the city into focus.

* * *

Two elements of Venice, stone and water, need a third to bind the whole into the extraordinary time-warp it inhabits: light. Dusk, dawn, vaporous or harshly overhead, the refraction of light on water dazzles or softly strokes, on stone creates tone, in shadow echoes suggestions that the past still hovers. A gondola appearing from the mist against an unfocused canal dissolves the centuries and we float free across the years. The light plays games. September evening turns the city into a molten shimmer, the palaces with flaming windows, a fishing boat on the lagoon silhouetted in horizonless copper.

Seeping fogs that creep and cloak increase the conviction that nothing is quite what it seems. This is the time that Venice seems to us most herself, private, wearing an appropriate half-veil, distances deceptive, distorted echoes following, the line between sky and water unclear. Morning, low tide, the dark recedes, the palaces emerge lace-shrouded, their foundations like ageing discoloured teeth protruding from receding gums, imbedded, insubstantial. The palaces seem to balance precariously on such indistinct bases, and we have to remember that we are standing on islands and sunken pylons, an absurd fantasy woven from influences both stolen and brought as gifts – Byzantine, Persian, Gothic – withdrawn into the closed mirage of winter's blur.

Campo San Maurizio, the light filtered pink, the night rain trapped on fluid flagstones. A few birds hopeful. In this light the Gothic windows are icing sugar, two-dimensional theatre scenery. As the day grows, so form will return, the square will have movement, the ground will dry, the fantasy backcloth will be taken for granted again. For this canvas, shown on pages 67 and 68, we wanted the ephemeral effect of that early light, and instead of the harsh time-ravages on the buildings, we preferred to show their fragility, a façade of frayed fabric instead of stone. The stitches cling to the canvas like fragments plucked from the walls, almost bricks, but not quite, perhaps more like stars, the shadowy interiors soft, the arches barely structured. As the light moves, different patches are thrown into relief – scatterings of Hungarian stitches, patches of satin stitch, everything changes with the movement of light.

In summer, the heat becomes sultry, weighted, too heavy to rise from the warren of streets. The smells hover: coffee, baking, garlic frying for *ragù*, different times of day heralding different smells. Thomas Mann wrote: 'The air was so heavy that all the manifold smells wafted out of houses, shops and cookshops – smells of oil, perfumery and so forth – hung low, like exhalations, not dissipating. Cigarette smoke seemed to stand in the air, it drifted so slowly away.' For those of us who love Venice, even the smell of a drain elsewhere can create a nostalgic smile.

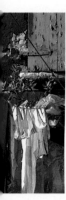

GERANIUMS

Window boxes of geraniums — turquoise and bottle green shutters, lace wafting, the walls flaking to show the brickwork skeleton beneath. Venetian geraniums, protected in the narrow streets and canals, behind balustrading and recessed against walls, continue to bloom until late in the year. The canvas is worked almost entirely in tent stitch, with just the blooms, leaves and wrought iron in simple stitchery for emphasis.

Previous page: The Geraniums photographed amid some dramatic windows in the Castello area.

Finished size of design
28×36cm (11×14in)

Yarns
Anchor tapisserie wool

	390 stone 3 skeins		611 scarlet 1 skein
	3057 beige 4 skeins		215 green 2 skeins
	421 peach 4 skeins		263 dark green 2 skeins
	498 mushroom 3 skeins		401 grey 4 skeins
	741 terracotta 2 skeins		3050 dark turquoise 2 skeins
	350 rust 2 skeins		3197 peacock 3 skeins
	499 cinnamon 3 skeins		3195 turquoise 2 skeins
	335 red 1 skein		402 white 2 skeins

Canvas
14-gauge white mono de luxe
Size: 38×48cm (15×19in)

Other materials
Tapestry needle, size 20
Ruler or tape measure
Masking tape for binding the canvas
Sharp scissors for cutting the canvas
Embroidery scissors
Sharp HB pencil or fine permanent
    marker in a suitable colour
Eraser

Following the chart
Cut the canvas to size and bind the edges with masking tape. The design does not have to be marked out on the canvas; just follow the colour chart on page 64. Remember that the squares represent the canvas inter-sections, not the holes. Each square represents one tent stitch.

The chart is divided up into units of 10 squares by 10 squares to make it easier to follow. Before beginning to stitch, it may be helpful to mark out your canvas in similar units of 10 squares by 10 squares with an HB pencil or permanent marker in a suitable colour. Also, we suggest marking the top of the canvas so that if you turn the canvas while you are stitching, you will still know where the top is.

The colours on the chart are shown stronger than the actual yarn colours to make them easier to see. The corresponding yarns are given in the colour key.

Stitches used
TENT stitch (1)
Optional:
SATIN stitch (3)
STEM stitch (8)
For stitch instructions, see pages 144 and 145.

Stitching the design
The whole thread of tapestry wool has been used throughout.

Begin in any area you wish. It might be easiest to start at the top right-hand corner, 4–5cm (1½–2in) in from the corner, working from one block of colour to another.

As you will see, we have stitched most of the design in TENT stitch (1) with just a few exceptions, which are worked in stitchery. The whole design can be worked using TENT stitch (1) throughout, but for those who are a little more ambitious, the flowers, leaves and wrought iron can be left until the end and then blocked in with SATIN stitch (3). The horizontal lines on the shutters are sewn using STEM stitch (8) and the stems of the leaves and flowers are also sewn in STEM stitch (8). Refer to the diagram below and the colour photograph of the framed picture for the stitch direction.

Making up instructions
When the design has been sewn, the needlepoint may need to be stretched back into shape (see stretching instructions on page 139). You may prefer to take your needlepoint to a professional picture framer who will also stretch it for you.

Yarns

Anchor tapisserie wool

390 stone 3 skeins	**421** peach 4 skeins	**499** cinnamon 3 skeins	**611** scarlet 1 skein
3057 beige 4 skeins	**498** mushroom 3 skeins	**335** red 1 skein	**215** green 2 skeins

350 rust 2 skeins	**741** terracotta 2 skeins	**263** dark green 2 skeins	**3197** peacock 3 skeins
401 grey 4 skeins	**3195** turquoise 2 skeins	**3050** dark turquoise 2 skeins	**402** white 2 skeins

Venice is described as a body, the buildings the muscles, the main canals the veins, the tiny side canals the capillaries. To move house in Venice is three times the price of Rome or Milan – the equivalent to the removal van may not be able to draw up to your watery back door. In summer the humidity, in winter the rheumatism, are facts of life. The elderly lower baskets on string from their windows and stairwells, to lift necessities. The very young and the very old are jolted up and down the uneven bridges in their wheelchairs, with a force guaranteed to rattle the first and last teeth from the head.

As well as the diverse architecture, Venetians themselves are a glorious mix of bloods and cultures. The people of Chioggia, Pellestrina and Burano have a different look from the Venetians of the city, and the same surnames on the island are very common. To differentiate, they'll add a nickname – for example: Cold Slippers Scarpa. The Venetian accent is lazy, the words get softly swallowed, and they'll write Venexia instead of Venezia because it sounds gentler that way.

Venice is full of details that she claims as her own. The posters in Padua or Ravenna may also advertise a concert, soap powder, a municipal notice, but the walls they are stuck to in Venice are unlike other walls, shredding in harmony with the city's crumbling streets. Venice has street names that are often a delight, written as they are in the Italian equivalent of Shakespearean English (a folly of the municipality). Many are connected with textiles – the Woolwashers' Archway, Dyers' Bridge, Garments Passage. There are many squares, but only one Piazza; the rest are called *campo*, meaning 'field' because that is what they were.

Street titles are unique to Venice: *calle*, like alley, is a narrow street; *fondamenta* is a paved strip at the edge of a canal; *sottoportego* is a low arch under a building, leading to a *calle*. *Piscina* is not a swimming pool, but the site of a pond, thus Sottoportego della Piscina is a low archway under a building leading to a covered street where an old pond used to be. As with the Venetian dialect, names are also sometimes slurred together. We were told of a stunning example of a beadwork *baldacchino*, a canopy, at the Church of Santi Giovanni e Paolo. After great frustration we found the church, but written as San Zanipolo. Clarity is not a virtue revered by Venetians, and the code must be cracked.

* * *

We love the city's doorways. The promise behind a closed door, like the cover of an unopened book. Let's take a doorway in the Cannaregio section. The door is arched, the windows on either side echo its shape and are pressed as close as they can be. One iron grille has a piece of string tied to it. One window has a metal staple angled like a sticking plaster over an aged eyebrow. The brickwork is, of course, Venetian red, and little of the plasterwork is left on top of the bricks, as if a palette-knife had scraped a bit of icing across.

Reflections. Before the day starts, the side canals duplicate the city with little distortion, mirrored railings barely tremor, sometimes the water line is hard to see. Then the inverted world becomes inhabited by quivering washing, gondolas, boats delivering and churning. Green predominates, stirred with brown and red and silver sky, the sun shimmers gold confetti and turns the reflected city into a sublime Monet canvas.

At night the mirror is bottomless black, the gondolas moored, the city silent. Then a motor boat with its lights off and carrying the equivalent of six Hell's Angels shrieks round the corner, under the bridge where we stand, smashing the mirror into chaos. What else can you do for excitement in Venice at night?

* * *

We were once guests in a house alongside the Santa Maria della Salute (which for us holds the distinction of being the coldest church in Venice). On the outside, the house was crumbling horribly, victim of salt and Mestre's industrial pollution, which in a year could corrode paintwork very efficiently. On the inside it was exquisite, what estate agents truly could call a 'bijou residence'. On the very top floor was a trellised roof garden that looked across to the Salute, and from that closeness we could see weeds sprouting from the dome. The city is full of incongruities. And someone had written below: Beware Falling Angels.

Above: Needlepoint based on reflections in water.

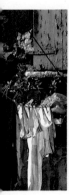

Now. Portray this door, not with pen or brush or words, but with needle and thread. It is slower, certainly, the canvas or linen and yarns create their own restrictions and have their own will. We all see things differently, so we select what we want to show, and this will be different for all of us, and reflect our feeling for the city. The same picture, dependent on your mood, can be smiling or sad. One day you may accentuate the beautiful patina of age and warmth of the door, on another the wood may simply be bleached from neglect. The steps may show a history of living, or they may simply be crumbling.

There may be fifty colours in the terracotta bricks, from ash and umber on the ground to pink and silver at the window ledge – or simply six shades of terracotta and grey. The picture seems deceptively simple: a doorway, two windows, brickwork. But remember, there are overtones in the heart as well as the eye, and although there is dignity in those centuries of stone, there is also debris trapped between window and grille. We can choose to ignore or emphasize. The decision, and result, will be unique. Again, do the only thing that can be done in Venice: regard the subject as an eccentric old relative, with its frailties, faults and charm.

If working from a photograph you can enlarge the picture and then trace the outlines through on to canvas with a waterproof pen; paint freehand on to canvas or linen; or mark on to linen – details of how to do this are on page 138.

There are three ways of choosing colours. The first is to dip randomly into a box of yarn oddments left from other projects, with a flexible idea of what you want, rummaging until something jumps out which could be the key to unlock a whole platoon of kindred colours. If your box represents years of gathered colours in tones you gravitate towards, you will usually be able to find just what you need.

The second way, for new needlepointers, is to decide in theory what colours are needed. But be flexible, if this is to be the creative fun it can be. Break the picture into groups, see where the colours can overlap. If you really want to 'paint' with your needle, use fine crewel wool and mix a needleful of blended colours, a bit of this from that brick, a little bit of that from the door, to make the transition between areas gentle and to give you dozens of colour permutations. In brickwork you could try keeping one strand of a basic colour common to all the bricks, and from that constant base wonderful harmonies can be achieved and the whole cannot fail to blend. Imagine a rogue maroon sock in the wrong machine wash. Every item would take the maroon sock differently, depending on the fabric and colour. Next time this happens, enjoy seeing how harmonious every item is, with that basic common link running (literally) through everything. Sustain this enjoyment as you admire your pink tennis whites. So, be approximately guided by your basic groups, but if something else catches your eye – metallic thread, twisted pearl cotton for lustre – incorporate it, because it is that spontaneity that will make your work unique and give you the confidence that this can work! When you have picked all the colours, spread them out and make a pared-down choice and then do the difficult bit. Keep your hands off the yarns until you get home.

The third way to choose yarns is similar to the second, but you have to own the needlework shop. You can then feel like a gourmet with an open cheque in Harrods Food Hall.

Left: Partially worked doorway design on canvas.
Opposite: Campo San Maurizio – the crumbling brickwork
is suggested by using different yarns and stitches.

CAMPO SAN MAURIZIO

This picture is worked mainly in tent stitch, with a few random patches of stitchery included to give the feeling of crumbling brickwork. The design shows the square in surreal pink early light, rain on the flagstones, a few pigeons reflected in the puddles. Wool and coton perlé are used on the façade of the buildings, and silver metallic thread for the reflections.

Finished size of design
28×38cm (11×15in)

Yarns
Appleton's tapestry wool
75cm (30in) lengths

962 grey 30 lengths		**981** beige 18 lengths	
883 heather 42 lengths		**221** mid terracotta 63 lengths	
602 mauve 36 lengths		**202** orchid 66 lengths	
204 terracotta 21 lengths		**991** white 24 lengths	

DMC coton perlé No.3

415 grey 3 skeins		**739** cream 4 skeins	

Madeira metallic thread
5010
silver
1 skein

Canvas
14-gauge white mono de luxe
Size: 38×48cm (15×19in)

Other materials
Tapestry needle, size 20
Ruler or tape measure
Masking tape for binding the canvas
Sharp scissors for cutting the canvas
Embroidery scissors
Sharp HB pencil or fine permanent marker in a suitable colour
Eraser

Following the chart
Cut the canvas to size and bind the edges with masking tape. The design does not have to be marked out on the canvas; just follow the colour chart opposite. Remember that the squares represent the canvas intersections, not the holes. Each square represents one tent stitch.

The chart is divided up into units of 10 squares by 10 squares to make it easier to follow. Before beginning to stitch, it may be helpful to mark out your canvas in similar units of 10 squares by 10 squares with an HB pencil or permanent marker in a suitable colour. Also, we suggest marking the top of the canvas so that if you turn the canvas while you are stitching, you will still know where the top is.

The colours on the chart are shown stronger than the actual yarn colours to make them easier to see. The corresponding yarns are given in the colour key.

Stitches used
TENT stitch (1)
Optional:
SATIN stitch (3)
CROSS stitch (9) over two threads
DOUBLE CROSS stitch (10)
HUNGARIAN stitch (14)
For stitch instructions, see pages 144, 146 and 147.

Stitching the design
The whole thread of tapestry wool and of coton perlé is used throughout. The silver thread is used double.

Begin in any area you wish. It might be easiest to start at the top right-hand corner, 4–5cm (1½–2in) in from the corner, working from one block of colour to another.

You can sew the whole design in TENT stitch (1) throughout. Alternatively, you can work certain areas of the design in stitchery to give an added dimension: see numbers on the chart for which stitch goes where, and refer to the colour photograph of the framed picture for the direction of the stitches.

The grillework on the windows is in CROSS stitch (9) over two threads. Parts of the stonework are in SATIN stitch (3), HUNGARIAN stitch (14) or DOUBLE CROSS stitch (10) sewn randomly. If you feel you would like to experiment with more stitchery, feel free to do so – or you may prefer to use just TENT stitch.

Making up instructions
When the design has been sewn, the needlepoint may need to be stretched back into shape (see stretching instructions on page 139). You may prefer to take your needlepoint to a professional picture framer who will also stretch it for you.

*This page: Examples of the richness of Venetian colours
and the visual pleasures hidden around every corner – the
most modest of courtyard water-wells, the dignity of simple
arches, the patchwork of Venice's rooftops.
Opposite: The Golden Street Scene – a curved walkway,
houses in ochre shades and late summer warmth, in a
setting echoing the tones of a Venetian autumn.*

The colours of Venice are rich in depth and age and tone. Everywhere Venetian red, the gamut of Venetian red from tired end-of-season roses, to vibrant just-squeezed-from-the-tube fresh – not terracotta, not crimson, somewhere between, washing the city, either singing or whispering, always looking as though it will leave pigment on your hands if you rub it. Between the reds, there is yellow ochre, earthy fruity pigment.

For the Golden Street Scene opposite, we wanted to show those ochres, intensified to give the look seen as storm clouds fly, the exaggerated yellows, siennas and lichen-coloured peelings of paint, the angle of light, gashes of white. Worked tiny, to create the feeling of peering into an old painting, clouded with age and varnish.

The street scene was inspired by a painting by Unterberger, painted as the year waned for such glowing mellow light. It was this aspect of radiance and ochres, and fading warmth, that we wanted to convey. Venetian shadows are rarely such simple browns, they are mottled mauve and grey, and on the canvas the colours were reworked many times until they disappeared as rich hollows, the negatives that give form to the positives.

All Venice is canals or *calli*, all have windows, shutters, wrought iron, and how many different bridges and balustrades can there be? Only thousands. One late October evening, walking along the Zattere, it was quite magical to find ourselves by chance crossing a bridge and stepping into the golden street scene, so familiar in paint and canvas, but not in reality. There was always the thought that Herr Unterberger had used artistic licence and that the painting was a glorious composite, but here it was: intact, perfect. The passage of time had only added the bonus of satellite dishes.

* * *

After rain, old Venetian rooftiles are nothing short of spectacular. They look like the carefully organized scales of a technicolour armadillo, in every tone of copper and moss green, every blue from grey to mauve, terracottas from apricot to rust. Where they are broken, extra tiles are squeezed in, looking like deformed, encrusted ingrown toenails.

GOLDEN STREET SCENE

Inspired by a painting by Unterberger, the glowing golden scene suggests the mellow evening light of late summer. The houses with their wrought-iron balconies and arched windows curve along the side of a canal, a mother sits with her children in a doorway and a couple stroll by.

Finished size of design
18 × 31cm (7 × 12¼in)

Canvas
18-gauge white mono de luxe
Size: 28 × 41cm (11 × 16in)

Other materials
Tapestry needle, size 22
Ruler or tape measure
Masking tape for binding the canvas
Sharp scissors for cutting the canvas
Embroidery scissors
Sharp HB pencil or fine permanent
   marker in a suitable colour
Eraser

Following the chart
Cut the canvas to size and bind the edges with masking tape. The design does not have to be marked out on the canvas; just follow the colour chart opposite. Remember that the squares represent the canvas inter-sections, not the holes. Each square represents one tent stitch.

The chart is divided up into units of 10 squares by 10 squares to make it easier to follow. Before beginning to stitch, it may be helpful to mark out your canvas in similar units of 10 squares by 10 squares with an HB pencil or permanent marker in a

suitable colour. Also, we suggest marking the top of the canvas so that if you turn the canvas while you are stitching, you will still know where the top is.

The colours on the chart are shown stronger than the actual yarn colours to make them easier to see. The corresponding yarns are given in the colour key.

Stitches used
TENT stitch (1)
Optional:
SPLIT BACK stitch (6)
CROSS stitch (9) over two threads
For stitch instructions, see pages 144, 145 and 146.

Stitching the design
Use two strands of crewel wool throughout.

Begin in any area you wish. It might be easiest to start work at the top right-hand corner, 4–5cm (1½–2in) in from the corner, working from one block of colour to another.

You can sew the whole design in TENT stitch (1). Alternatively, you can work certain details in stitchery to give an added dimension – refer to the colour photograph of the framed picture to see which stitch goes where. The balustrade on the balcony and the brown edging on the umbrella are both worked in SPLIT BACK stitch (6). The entire design is surrounded by CROSS stitch (9) over two threads.

Making up instructions
When the design has been sewn, the needlepoint may need to be stretched back into shape (see stretching instructions on page 139). You may prefer to take your needlepoint to a professional picture framer who will also stretch it for you.

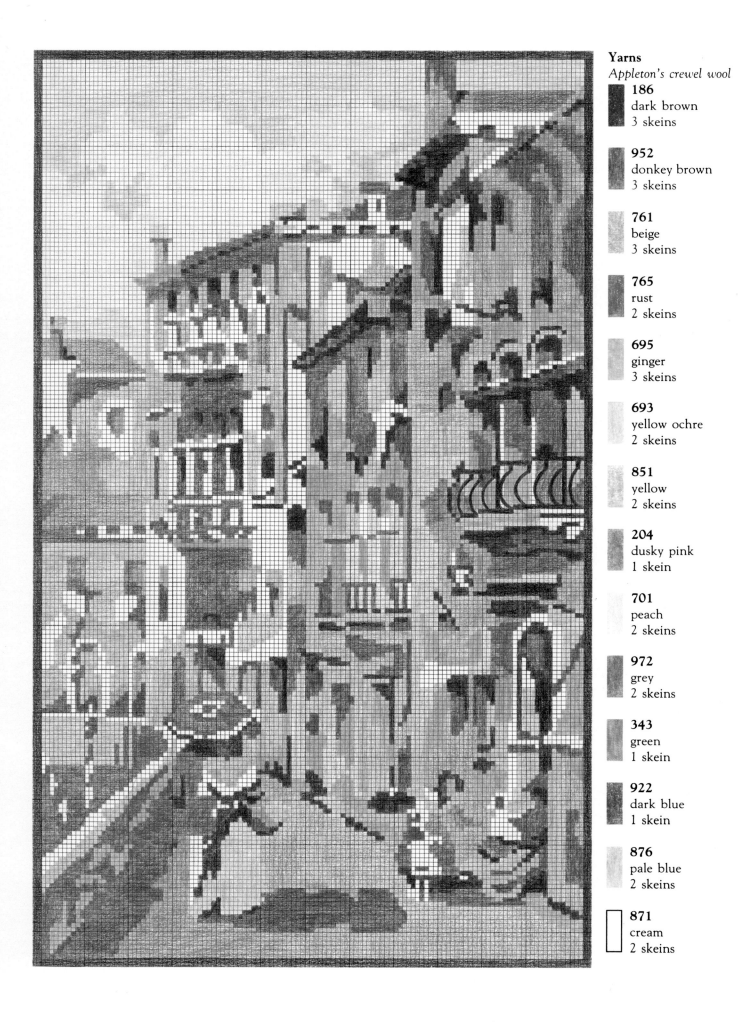

Yarns
Appleton's crewel wool

186
dark brown
3 skeins

952
donkey brown
3 skeins

761
beige
3 skeins

765
rust
2 skeins

695
ginger
3 skeins

693
yellow ochre
2 skeins

851
yellow
2 skeins

204
dusky pink
1 skein

701
peach
2 skeins

972
grey
2 skeins

343
green
1 skein

922
dark blue
1 skein

876
pale blue
2 skeins

871
cream
2 skeins

VENICE AND FOOD

The best place to think about food is around Rialto. The Rialto Bridge was always Venice's centre of commerce, and though the money market no longer flourishes, the fruit and fish markets do. The Bridge is one of the city's landmarks, and also has another significance. It is known, to a few intimates, as the place from where Shirley L. wants her ashes scattered as the evening sun sets (at the top of the steps on the San Bartolomeo side, facing Ca' Dolfin-Manin, which is appropriate because it's where the last Doge removed his crown saying, 'Take it, I shall not be needing it again') with many hosannas, and later a glass raised to an absent stylish sister-in-law at her favourite restaurant.

Early morning always seems the fastest time around the Bridge, a speeded-up silent movie, the silver city unfocused, people being disgorged from the *vaporetti*, some into Rialto cafés for coffee and sweet bread eaten silently standing, sometimes a cognac against the chill, shop shutters being cranked open, barrows jolted down stone steps, boats disappearing in dawn vapour. Then cross into the market, and feel your eyes immediately become taste-buds!

Boxes and stalls of *rucola*, sprays of rosemary, baby beetroot, tomatoes with the indentations of pumpkins, gold courgette flowers piled into honeycombs, ballerina mushrooms in their great tutus, asparagus trussed into straitjackets, fruits coated with misty bloom, artichokes the size of a forefinger and thumb touching. Shops crowded with salamis and cheeses and kaleidoscope jars of pickled vegetables; Rizzo Fernando's shop where they have been making and selling paintbox pasta for seventy years — the red is beetroot, the black cuttlefish, the green spinach, the shades of brown are mushroom, curry and chocolate . . . and on to the fish market, an architectural delight, the arches sheltering the generations of fishsellers whose mornings start at 3.30 and who must rejoice when the winter recedes and the lighter mornings start again.

We never know why the fish market always puts us in such a wonderful mood; it's hard to understand why something so slimy, and often still writhing and twitching, should be so cheerful. The colours, the iridescence, are a feast. And it is such sublime slime! Things move as imperceptibly as kinetic sculpture — a black lobster claw giving a slow benediction to his fellows on the slab they share; shells in satisfying twisting knots and textures, pink and grey in green nets; regimented rows of crayfish, tidy as a nursery; beautiful mullet and hideous spider-crabs — the *granzeola* we so love; trays of Creatures from the Black Lagoon. And piles of squid in pools of ink, seeming to be barely solid — do we imagine they will liquefy as we watch? Great cross-sections of bloody tuna, and fish striped pink and peach, delicate, transparent, luminous, scaled. Tread warily, sweet ladies, among the bag-toting mammas with their demanding elbows, before the sun is overhead and the market evaporates.

* * *

There are special dishes for celebrations, for example, the Festival of Redentore — when a bridge of boats is built to give thanks to the Church of the Redeemer for the end of the plague in 1577 — is celebrated with duck and marinated sardines and onions. In one of Goldoni's plays he copies a menu for *Giovedi Grasso* (the last Thursday before Lent) in 1762: *ravioli* stuffed with meat and served with cinnamon, butter and sugar, then three meat dishes: boiled meat with horseradish, stuffed turkey with radicchio, horsemeat marinated with spices with *rucola*. Then pastry and custard. Then probably a wet towel on the head in a darkened room. The most popular Venetian sweet is *fritola*, usually associated with the last days of Carnival, and so respected that the *fritoleri* had their own guild. A *fritola* is simple: flour, grappa or aniseed flavouring, raisins and pine seeds, fried in oil. Other Veneto variations have apple, marrow, semolina or polenta.

Wild game used to be very plentiful in the Lagoon: wild duck, bullfinches, coots, which were part of common diet. A greasy seagull does not compare.

* * *

The Shells cushion overleaf has two panels, mirror images like an open bi-valve, with scallops, murex, clams, in the iridescent colours they look in the overhead market lights, soft pinks, beige, yellow, cream, shades of blue, bordered by panels of flowers and ribbon, interlaced with seaweed. The cushion sits on a vast stone bench, as if just washed up from the sea. The debris that the tide brought up, stones and starfish, bask in the sun. The English preoccupation with fish and chips in newspaper seems to have crept into the photograph, but the newspaper is *Il Giorno*, and each piece contains a shell.

Above: Watercolour sketches for a needlepoint design.

SHELLS

Murex, scallops, clams, in iridescent pinks, blues and ochres, are needle-pointed in mirror images like an open shell and bordered by panels of scrolls interlaced with seaweed.

Finished size of design
37×31cm (14½×12in)

Yarns
Appleton's tapestry wool
75cm (30in) lengths

924
dark blue
36 lengths

301
fawn
45 lengths

741
pale blue
54 lengths

473
gold
72 lengths

222
dark pink
24 lengths

471
yellow
48 lengths

221
pink
36 lengths

841
pale yellow
45 lengths

991
white
81 lengths

Canvas
14-gauge white interlock
Size: 47×41cm (18½×16in)

Other materials
Tapestry needle, size 20
Ruler or tape measure
Masking tape for binding the canvas
Sharp scissors for cutting the canvas
Embroidery scissors
Sharp HB pencil or fine permanent
    markers in suitable colours
Eraser
Tracing paper and fine black marker

Marking the canvas and following the chart
Cut the canvas to size and bind the edges with masking tape. The whole design does not have to be marked out on the canvas; just follow the colour chart opposite and then trace the shell design for the two panels from page 153, as described on the next page. Remember that the squares represent the canvas inter-sections, not the holes. Each square represents one tent stitch.

The chart is divided up into units of 10 squares by 10 squares to make it easier to follow. Before beginning to stitch, it may be helpful to mark out your canvas in similar units of 10 squares by 10 squares with an HB pencil or permanent marker in a suitable colour. Also, we suggest

marking the top of the canvas so that
if you turn the canvas while you are
stitching, you will still know where
the top is.

The colours on the chart are
shown stronger than the actual yarn
colours to make them easier to see.
The corresponding yarns are given in
the colour key.

Stitches used
TENT stitch (1)
SATIN stitch (3)
STEM stitch (8)
For stitch instructions, see pages 144
and 145.

Stitching the design
Use the whole thread of tapestry
wool. TENT stitch (1) is used throughout with the exception of the two
shell panels where SATIN stitch (3)
and STEM stitch (8) are also used.

Begin with the TENT stitch (1) in
any area you wish. It might be easiest

to start at the top right-hand corner,
4–5cm (1½–2in) in from the corner,
working from one block of colour to
another.

When you have finished stitching
from the chart, it is necessary to
trace the shells on to the panels. As
you will see, there is only one outline
on page 153; simply take two tracings
of this shell panel using tracing paper
and a fine black marker. Reverse the
second tracing. Trace them on to the
canvas with a permanent marker in a
suitable colour, centring the tracings.
Follow the curved lines freely, ignoring the canvas grid.

If you are experienced it is not
necessary to trace the fine lines,
which are a guide to show where the
colours on the shells change. These
fine lines can be disregarded or can
be put on afterwards, freehand, in a
different colour. A beginner may
need to trace the fine lines – do this
in a different colour.

The numbers on the coloured artwork refer to the stitch numbers and
the arrows show the direction of the
stitches. Look at the photograph of
the made-up cushion and the coloured
artwork to show you which colour
goes where. Remember, this is a
guide; don't be restricted by it and
feel free to experiment.

The shells are worked in TENT
stitch (1) and SATIN stitch (3) with
outlining in STEM stitch (8). The
background is worked in white TENT
stitch (1) throughout.

Making up instructions
When the design has been sewn, the
needlepoint may need to be stretched
back into shape (see stretching instructions on page 139). Then make
it up into a cushion of your choice as
shown on pages 140–1.

FRUIT URN

We associate Venice with stone and water, but hidden behind high walls and rusted gates are private gardens, reclusive and shadowed, providing a soft and unexpected contrast to the stone of the city. The Fruit Urn shows an overgrown alcove in such a garden, with pomegranates and grapes, cherries and plums, tendrils of leaves and the patina of verdigris on the urn all contriving a rich Renaissance look.

Finished size of design
34×40cm (13½×15½in)

Yarns
Appleton's tapestry wool
75cm (30in) lengths

715
plum
18 lengths

645
sea green
48 lengths

765
chestnut
18 lengths

344
grass green
42 lengths

125
dark coral
18 lengths

355
fern green
72 lengths

205
coral
12 lengths

543
leaf green
27 lengths

695
ochre
18 lengths

251A
lime
64 lengths

472
gold
27 lengths

331
pale lime
60 lengths

348
dark olive
36 lengths

996
pale yellow
9 lengths

Canvas
14-gauge white mono de luxe
Size: 40×47cm (15½×18½in)

Other materials
Tapestry needle, size 20
Ruler or tape measure
Masking tape for binding the canvas
Sharp scissors for cutting the canvas
Embroidery scissors
Sharp HB pencil or fine permanent
   marker in a suitable colour
Eraser

Following the chart
Cut the canvas to size and bind the edges with masking tape. The design does not have to be marked out on the canvas; just follow the colour chart opposite. Remember that the squares represent the canvas inter-sections, not the holes. Each square represents one tent stitch.

The chart is divided up into units of 10 squares by 10 squares to make it easier to follow. Before beginning to stitch it may be helpful to mark out your canvas in similar units of 10 squares by 10 squares with an HB pencil or permanent marker in a suitable colour. Also, we suggest marking the top of the canvas so that if you turn it while stitching, you will still know where the top is.

The colours on the chart are shown stronger than the actual yarn colours to make them easier to see.

The corresponding yarns are given in the colour key.

Stitches used
TENT stitch (1) is used throughout. For stitch instructions, see page 144.

Stitching the design
The whole thread of tapestry wool is used throughout. Begin in any area you wish. It might be easiest to start at the top right-hand corner, 4–5cm (1½–2in) from the corner, working from one block of colour to another.

Making up instructions
When the design has been sewn, the needlepoint may need to be stretched back into shape (see stretching in-structions on page 139). You may prefer to take your needlepoint to a professional picture framer who will also stretch it for you.

Together and not together, by coincidence or perhaps not, for us Harry's Bar has always been a place for occasions – to celebrate marriage, birthdays, maybe just the need for indulgence, and our best indulgences happen at Harry's, alongside Confessions, Traumas and Happinesses. However much we enjoy the other Cipriani restaurants: the Locanda on Torcello, Harry's Dolci on Giudecca (not a fun part of Venice on a bleak wintry night), it is to Harry's that we have gravitated for over twenty years to celebrate, overall, friendship and food. The rest are ephemera, anyway.

The Harry of the name was Harry Pickering, an American whom Giuseppe Cipriani helped financially and they later went into partnership together. Arrigo, Giuseppe's son who runs Harry's and claims to be the only person named after a bar, says that had there been credit cards in those days, Harry Pickering would have charged his debts to Diners, there would have been no partnership and no Harry's Bar. And Arrigo would have been called Fabio, or Franco. Because of the famous Hemingway connection, some consider it almost a cliché to drink at Harry's, and particularly to drink a Bellini at Harry's. However, there are worse things than champagne and peach juice (we can easily name four thousand) and how many places are there in Venice where the customers can include a child drinking hot chocolate with her nanny, aristocracy and backpackers, sailors and ladies from Hartlepool, old money, new money and people writing needlepoint books?

* * *

The year Mara came into our lives, and through Mara Venetian home cooking, was the year we really began Glorafilia. We took a house in Selsea in East Sussex, installed Mara in the kitchen, designed our first collection of printed canvases, all sewed samples and listened to Neil Diamond's *Love at the Greek* all summer. Jason and Sorel were five, Tamsin was one, and in memory spent many weeks sitting in a washing-up bowl, trusting us that this was a swimming pool. Every evening, tide permitting, we would walk on the vast beach, the two older children like puppies, Tamsin a disgruntled roly-poly in red wellingtons and Pre-Raphaelite curls, not sure that this English mud was supposed to be fun. And every evening we came back to Mara's *risi e bisi*, or *risotto con spinaci*, or Venetian Russian salad full of pickled cauliflower, or *ragù* that used the same ingredients as our ragout but had the added indefinable ingredient of being stirred by an Italian hand. At weekends our men drove down and we became carnivores, a slab of cow, a great lamb thigh, that Mara would sadly sigh over, and then on Monday the glorious Venetian comfort food would reappear.

That was many years ago. Alison has since become the fourth Glorafilia child, the dumpling Tamsin is now a svelte young woman taller than her mother, the curls grew straight, and none of us can hear *Love at the Greek* without the Selsea association of Mara and her wonderful food. Her *gnocchi* were a disaster – even the waste disposal rejected them – but her *risi e bisi*? *Stupendo!*

* * *

Cross St Mark's Square, with the Basilica behind you, walking down on the left past the lace and tortoiseshell shops under the colonnades, and you will come to Caffè Florian. In the summer throngs drink espresso and Campari to the strains of 'Moon River' and 'Memories', in the winter the duck boards straddle the square for when the *aqua alta*, the high tide, floods the paving stones, making crossing a little like following the Yellow Brick Road, Oz's Emerald City replaced by one of Gothic grey dampness. Opposite is Quadri's, which has fine paintings, but none of the decayed magic of Florian. You don't go to Florian because you are thirsty or want to eat excellent Sacher Torte, or because you feel like paying exorbitantly for either. You go to Florian to sit on the banquettes among the frescoes and mirrors and frothy chandeliers, where the ghosts of Byron, George Sand, Goldoni, Goethe, Wagner and Casanova sit, and to inhale the atmosphere of years of commerce, gossip, discreet and indiscreet liaisons and aromas of coffee and spices.

The history of the Venetian coffee houses has been long: women were at one time forbidden, then later granted entry although only at certain times of year provided they wore a mask; frenzied gambling took hold, then begging; merchants conducted business, craftsmen sealed commissions. Florian was opened in 1720 in two small rooms, not the warren of opulence it is today. Customers took their own little heaters and wrapped themselves around them in their cloaks. Thirty years later it had grown to four rooms and as well as coffee house was a collection point for lost property, distribution centre for newspapers and later, expanded further, a headquarters for revolutionary meetings and a little field hospital, as well as the focal point for Venice's hedonistic society life.

Today Florian is a jewel in a city of set-pieces. It is where the poseurs of Carnival, the *mascheri*, are to be seen in February – and where else could be as appropriate? Each room is painted with its own identity, Greek, Chinese, Turkish, Persian. There is a decadent weary-courtesan air about Florian – all the murals and ceilings are behind glass, making the whole place rather precious, preserved, time-warped. In 1858 it was restored from top to bottom to be as we see it today. The Viennese writer, Karl Hernod, said:

> Europe is the most beautiful part of the world, Italy the most beautiful part of Europe, Venice the most beautiful part of Italy, St Mark's Square the most beautiful square in Venice, Florian the most beautiful café in the square. So I am drinking my moka in the most beautiful place in the world.

One of the most noticeable things about Florian's distinct façade is not the shaped beadings or decoration, but the reflections in the glass; the arches and windows of the Procuratie Vecchie opposite are thrown back, often with the distortion of a hall of mirrors – a reminder that this coffee house could be nowhere else on earth. And superimposed on these reflections are the inside images of the café, the frilly wall-lights, a profiled figure, a hatted and furred dowager with her elderly son, holding his cigarette between his third and fourth finger.

FLORIAN

Caffè Florian – a jewel in a city of set-pieces – was Europe's first coffee house and, with the architecture of Piazza di San Marco reflected in its windows, reminds us that we couldn't be anywhere but Venice.

Finished size of design
27 × 37cm (10½ × 14½in)

Canvas
14-gauge white mono de luxe
Size: 37 × 47cm (14½ × 18½in)

Other materials
Tapestry needle, size 20
Ruler or tape measure
Masking tape for binding the canvas
Sharp scissors for cutting the canvas
Embroidery scissors
Sharp HB pencil or fine permanent
   marker in a suitable colour
Eraser

Following the chart
Cut the canvas to size and bind the edges with masking tape. The design does not have to be marked out on the canvas; just follow the colour chart opposite. Remember that the squares represent the canvas intersections, not the holes. Each square represents one tent stitch.

The chart is divided up into units of 10 squares by 10 squares to make it easier to follow. Before beginning to stitch, it may be helpful to mark out your canvas in similar units of 10 squares by 10 squares with an HB pencil or permanent marker in a suitable colour. Also, we suggest marking the top of the canvas so that if you turn the canvas while you are stitching, you will still know where the top is.

The colours on the chart are shown stronger than the actual yarn colours to make them easier to see. The corresponding yarns are given in the colour key.

Stitches used
TENT stitch (1)

Optional
◙ SATIN stitch (3)
☑ SPLIT BACK stitch (6)
◨ Vertical BRICK stitch (12) over two threads
For stitch instructions, see pages 144, 145 and 147.

Stitching the design
Use the whole thread of tapestry wool throughout. Where gold thread is needed, use two strands.

Begin in any area you wish. It might be easiest to start at the top right-hand corner, 4–5cm (1½–2in) in from the corner, working from one block of colour to another. If you intend to use stitchery for part of the design, work it after the TENT stitch.

You can sew the whole design in TENT stitch (1) throughout. Alternatively, you can work certain areas of the design in stitchery to give an added dimension: see symbols on the chart for which stitch goes where, and refer to the colour photograph of the framed picture for the direction of the stitches.

The lady's dress is worked in vertical BRICK stitch (12) over two threads, her hat and hair are in SATIN stitch (3) and SPLIT BACK stitch (6), her face and hands are in TENT stitch (1). The chair is in SPLIT BACK stitch (6) and SATIN stitch (3); the table in diagonal SATIN stitch (3) and TENT stitch (1). The tea things are in diagonal SATIN stitch (3). The gold handle on the door is in SPLIT BACK stitch (6) and SATIN stitch (3). The railings are also in SPLIT BACK stitch (6).

Making up instructions
When the design has been sewn, the needlepoint may need to be stretched back into shape (see instructions on page 139). You may prefer to take your needlepoint to a professional picture framer who will also stretch it.

Yarns

Appleton's
tapestry wool
75cm (30in) lengths

326
navy
36 lengths

321
blue
27 lengths

851
custard
12 lengths

765
ginger
24 lengths

302
biscuit
36 lengths

305
brown
27 lengths

125
plum
27 lengths

205
terracotta
6 lengths

204
coral
12 lengths

964
grey
36 lengths

291A
algae green
48 lengths

989
stone
72 lengths

877
cream
60 lengths

Astrella
metallic thread
gold
1 skein

FRUIT PLACEMAT AND NAPKIN

The placemat – or tray cloth – was inspired by the design on an exquisite waistcoat embroidered around 1750, showing a densely worked border of fruit and flowers in rich shades of coral, ochre, mauve and forest green. The matching napkin shows two pears stitched in the same glowing colours, hanging simply from a leafy branch.

Finished sizes
Placemat 45×32cm (17½×12½in)
Napkin 41cm (16in) square

Yarns
Anchor stranded cotton

361
creamy yellow
2 skeins

943
ochre
3 skeins

337
pale coral
3 skeins

5975
dark coral
4 skeins

5968
rust
2 skeins

894
pale pink
2 skeins

970
dark pink
2 skeins

871
pale mauve
2 skeins

873
dark mauve
2 skeins

358
brown
2 skeins

856
olive
3 skeins

216
pale green
4 skeins

218
dark green
3 skeins

Type of fabric
A close-weave fabric of your choice, preferably linen or cotton
Size: **Placemat** 51×38cm (20×15in)
       Napkin 47cm (18½in) square

Other materials
Chenille needle, size 24
Ruler or tape measure
Sharp scissors for cutting the fabric
Embroidery scissors
Sharp HB pencil or fine permanent marker in a suitable colour
Tracing paper and fine black marker
Eraser
Embroidery transfer pencil
Iron

Tracing the design

Trace the outline for the placemat from pages 154–5 on to the tracing paper using a fine black marker. If you are experienced it is not necessary to trace the fine lines, which are a guide to show where the colours on the fruit and leaves change. These fine lines can be disregarded or can be put on afterwards, freehand. A beginner may need to trace the fine lines after tracing the thick lines.

As you will see, only two sides of the placemat are shown. When you have traced the design on to the tracing paper, turn the tracing to the left twice (through 180 degrees) until the design forms an oblong with the outline in the book. Trace the design again, taking care with the positioning. You will now have the four sides interlocking together. Trace the motif for the napkin on to a separate piece of tracing paper.

Transferring the design on to the fabric

Method 1

This is an easier and quicker method, but you have to have a light box! Put the tracing on a light box and place the fabric for the placemat on the top, positioning it in the centre.

Trace the design using a fine permanent marker or an HB pencil. Repeat with the napkin.

Method 2

Turn your first tracing over and retrace the design for the placemat and the napkin on to another piece of tracing paper, using an embroidery transfer pencil. (If you don't turn your tracing over, you will get a mirror image of the design when you come to transfer it.) A transfer pencil can be used on natural fabrics such as cotton or linen, but not on polyester or acrylic. Make sure that the pencil has a fine point to avoid a thick line, which may be difficult to cover completely when you come to work the embroidery.

Set the iron to a moderate heat, but test a small part of the design on a piece of waste material first to determine the correct temperature required, as different fabrics require different temperatures. Iron the fabric for the placemat until a smooth surface is obtained. Place the design in the required position, centring it with the pencil side of the paper nearest the fabric, and iron over the design. It is important not to move the tracing paper as the impression will become blurred.

Repeat with the napkin.

Stitches used

LONG AND SHORT stitch (A)
SATIN stitch (B)
STEM stitch (C)
FRENCH KNOTS (D)

Stitching the design

Three strands of stranded cotton are used throughout. For the position and direction of the stitches, refer to the photograph of the made-up placemat and napkin on page 91. The coloured artwork below and right will show you which colour yarn goes where and the letters refer to the embroidery stitch diagrams on the opposite page, which will show you how to do the stitches.

The pears and some flowers and leaves are worked in LONG AND SHORT stitch (A). Some small berries, flowers and leaves are sewn in SATIN stitch (B), some flowers are outlined in STEM stitch (C) and the stems are also sewn in STEM stitch (C). Flower centres are a single FRENCH KNOT (D).

Making up instructions

After you have finished working the embroidery, press a double 1.3cm (½in) turning all round, mitring the corners. Machine or hand sew into place. Press firmly with an iron set to a moderate heat.

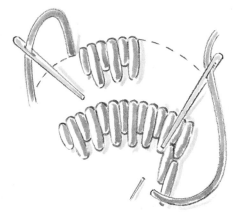

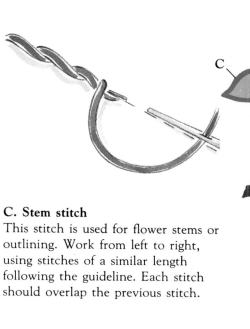

A. Long and short stitch

In the first row the stitches are alternately long and short. In the subsequent rows all stitches are of the same length. Begin at the centre of the outside edge. In second and subsequent rows stitch down through the embroidery and up into the linen – this will split the thread and create a smooth effect.

C. Stem stitch

This stitch is used for flower stems or outlining. Work from left to right, using stitches of a similar length following the guideline. Each stitch should overlap the previous stitch.

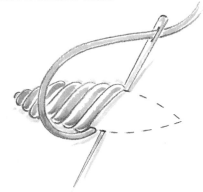

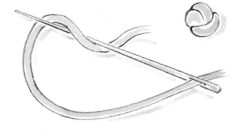

D. French knots

Hold the thread firmly with thumb and forefinger about 5cm (2in) from the point where the thread emerges from the fabric. Twist the needle only once round the thread in a clockwise direction and pull tightly. Insert the needle almost in the same place as it emerged and pull through to form a French knot. If a thicker French knot is required, use more strands of yarn.

B. Satin stitch

May be worked horizontally, vertically or diagonally – perfect for leaves. Take care when working this stitch to keep a straight edge and to sew with an even tension. Lay straight stitches closely together across the shape.

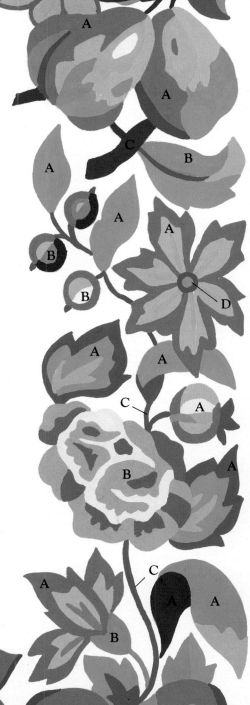

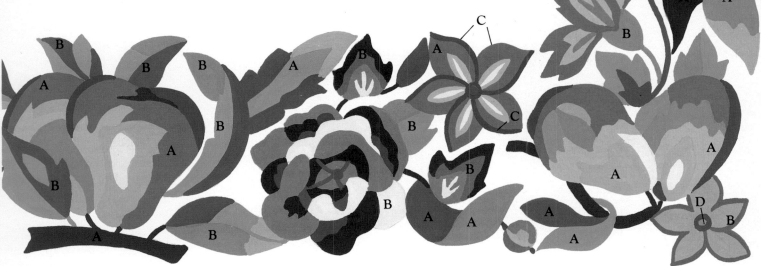

CARNIVAL

CARNIVAL

Masks. Masks with eyes . . . there is the fascination of the untold, the averted, the concealed shyness, the actor in all of us. The alternative, the clandestine, the promise behind the veil, the suggestion of something not as it seems. In Venice, Carnival is not the extrovert organized turmoil of Trinidad or Rio, it is a homage to a Venice past, a step into the corridor of memory, every February restaged. Heads turn in disbelief until the eye accepts. Are the masks, the lace, the walls swept with a velvet cape – the grim *Bautta* disappearing into an alleyway – really in the present or is the intoxicated mind deliciously distorting imagined spirits? It could happen nowhere but here, against a backcloth no set designer could contrive, jealously itself, host to fantasies limited only by the imagination. There is a wistfulness, a melancholia, a desire to 'play the mask' with an elegance mindful of tradition. Shameless poseurs parade, a child harlequin star-gazes, an emperor strides across an indistinct bridge, a drawn cloak shields a player from the light, flounces reflect on floating streets, a witch and magician dance by the glow of a lantern. A city that at all times echoes dreams, during Carnival becomes surreal street theatre with images back-projected on to aged walls. Byron said: 'and, after all, what is a lie? 'Tis but the truth in masquerade.'

Carnival has been a happening in Venice since the twelfth century, when *Giovedi Grasso* became the day celebrating a Venetian victory, interweaving myth, history and religion to glorify Justice. On the last Thursday before Lent in 1162, the Venetians overthrew Aquileia, the centuries-old enemy of the Republic. Ulrich the Patriarch, twelve clergy and seven hundred followers were taken prisoner and condemned to death in Venice. They were finally saved by the then Pope on condition that a symbolic humiliating tribute of a bull (for Ulrich), twelve pigs (for the clergy) and an appropriate number of loaves be sent to Venice annually. The celebrations for the procession of tributes included a bullfight in Piazza di San Marco, a 'battle' mass in the Basilica and other unsavoury practices, which were banned in 1520.

For centuries, the main stage of the celebrations was St Mark's Square: enormous 'theatrical machines' were erected, fireworks, human pyramids, men as angels 'flying' from the top of the Bell Tower. In 1786 Goethe described the Carnival:

During the daytime squares, canals, gondolas and palazzi are full of life as buyer and seller, beggar and boatman, housewife and lawyer offer something for sale, sing and gamble, shout and swear. In the evenings these same people go to the theatre to behold their actual life, presented with greater economy as make-believe, interwoven with fairy tales and removed from reality by masks, yet, in its characters and manners, the life they know. They are delighted, like children, shouting, clapping and generally making a din. From sunset to sunset, midnight to midnight, they are just the same.

In the Piazza, there were minuets danced, charlatans, snake charmers, musicians, tooth pullers, salesmen selling the oil of philosophy, glasses to see in the dark. There were tightrope walkers, elephants, leopards, waxwork museums, illuminated allegorical floats. Royalty and adventurers flocked to Venice, drawn by the frenetic life-style, the bull-hunting, the day and night *mascherate* – trains of thirty or forty costumed masked revellers snaking the city. The bewitchment.

Above: Carnival revellers as they are today.
Opposite: A fan, depicting Carnival in the eighteenth century – the entire fan, including the fretwork sticks, is worked in needlepoint.

The last Carnival under the Republic was in 1797, heedless of the international clouds that were to bring a dark future for the Serenissima. Venice, then no longer sovereign, but subject, continued Carnival, but the life-style of the city changed and it became an affair for a closer circle of people; the masked parades found their way inside the *palazzi*, invited to cheer up the parties there. The sinister black mantle of the *Bautta* became increasingly apparent, and the world of Carnival shrank to one of nostalgia and illusion. Seventy years were to pass before Venice recovered its lost image and, in 1867, a few months after Venice became united with the Kingdom of Italy, the streets again became full of pleasure-seekers.

It is almost impossible to pass shops in Venice without the visual bombardment of masks – the *Bautta*, mentioned before, with its veil, cloak and tricorn hat, Doctor Peste with his great beak to hold a nosegay to counter the stench of the city as he did his rounds . . . some kitsch, some exquisite and faithful to the *commedia dell'arte* from whence they came. Almost every civilization continues its romance with the mask. In antiquity, the Greek and Roman theatres were so huge that actors' faces could not be seen distinctly, so masks proportioned to the size of the theatre were worn. However, the concept of masks came into being long before then, perhaps as a childish impulse for change, perhaps to aspire to a god-like appearance, perhaps simply to frighten the horses (or fellow men). In theatre, people in general welcome that which they know. An audience responds to a familiar face rather than a new one and the mask is the easiest way to give permanence to a favourite character: this is the most likely reason that the traditional masks of the Italian comedy were conceived.

These *commedia dell'arte* masks neither laugh nor cry. They have enigmatic qualities on which the character can be stamped. The French say *jouer du masque* – the art of 'playing the mask' – because seen from different angles these masks can convey vastly different emotions. And the body becomes a new type of face, as with the ancient Greeks' 'gestures that speak a language, hands that have a mouth, fingers that speak voices'. The most famous Italian comedy playwrights, Gozzi and Goldoni, had differing views. Gozzi was a traditionalist and encouraged masks; Goldoni believed, very progressively, that masks 'interfered with the actors' performance and that nowadays the actor is required to have "soul" and the soul beneath the mask is as fire beneath ashes'.

The *commedia dell'arte* dated from the Renaissance, a fantasy-world peopled with picturesque characters: Harlequin, Columbine, Pierrot, Pulcinella, Scaramouche and Pantaloon; its origins were in Italy, but eventually took root all over Europe. As a travelling show it was described as: 'A droll spectacle to behold. There were a dozen people, as many actors as actresses, a prompter, a stage carpenter, a property man, eight menservants, four maids, nurses, children of all ages, dogs, cats, monkeys, parrots, birds, pigeons, a lamb – it was a Noah's Ark.'

Pierrot first seems to appear in an Italian company as early as the sixteenth century. He is always depicted as a servant, albeit a clever and influential one, an untangler of plot intrigues. Over the years and in different plays, his character developed until he became as we perceive him today: sensitive, wistful and lonely, emotionally appealing and a little melancholy. We love the gentleness of his image and, on page 102, show him alone and pensive, isolated within a complex border, the stream of life flowing at his feet . . . and have borrowed the diamonds on his costume from Harlequin, in artistic licence to waylay needle tedium!

* * *

The Fenice Theatre is a spectacular jewel of an opera house and in its heyday was where Venice's society gathered. Having a box at the Fenice had several uses. It was the most expedient way of seeing the rest of society since most people went most evenings. It also saved lighting and heating their homes. *La Traviata* was first performed there (and booed there) and though now, as then, it is Venice's main theatre, its offerings are sparse.

The starting point for our theatre design opposite and overleaf was the elaborate proscenium, swagged curtains and rather stilted grand figures of eighteenth-century prints and models. The simple device of the stripes in the background and contrasting curve of the seats in the foreground prevents visual indigestion from this over-the-top confection. The design is worked almost entirely in tent stitch, in places reversing the direction to keep the diagonal lines unbroken, and introducing some satin stitch to make the flounces smoother.

Left: Carnival as it was, in Piazza di San Marco.

COMMEDIA DELL'ARTE

*This design evokes the opulence of the Fenice Theatre in its heyday . . .
the elaborate proscenium, swagged curtains and stilted grand figures of
the eighteenth century.*

Finished size of design
31cm (12in) square

Yarns
DMC Medicis crewel wool

blanc
2 skeins

8168
rust
4 skeins

8109
mushroom
2 skeins

8800
pale blue
3 skeins

8328
pale yellow
4 skeins

8209
turquoise
3 skeins

8326
gold
3 skeins

8930
midnight blue
4 skeins

8505A
pale peach
3 skeins

8200
navy
4 skeins

8164
apricot
2 skeins

8508
dove grey
3 skeins

8166
terracotta
2 skeins

8507
dark grey
2 skeins

Canvas
18-gauge white mono de luxe
Size: 41cm (16in) square

Other materials
Tapestry needle, size 22
Ruler or tape measure
Masking tape for binding the canvas
Sharp scissors for cutting the canvas
Embroidery scissors
Sharp HB pencil or fine permanent
   marker in a suitable colour
Eraser

Following the chart
Cut the canvas to size and bind the
edges with masking tape. The design
does not have to be marked out on
the canvas; just follow the colour
chart shown opposite. Remember
that the squares of the chart
represent the canvas intersections,
not the holes. Each square represents
one tent stitch.

The chart is divided up into units
of 10 squares by 10 squares to make
it easier to follow. Before beginning
to stitch, it may be helpful to mark
out your canvas in similar units of
10 squares by 10 squares with an
HB pencil or permanent marker in a
suitable colour. Also, we suggest
marking the top of the canvas so that
if you turn it while stitching, you will
still know where the top is.

The colours on the chart are
shown stronger than the actual yarn
colours to make them easier to see.
The corresponding yarns are given in
the colour key.

Stitches used
TENT stitch (1)
Optional:
◩ Reversed TENT stitch (1)
◙ SATIN stitch (3)
◪ Vertical BRICK stitch (12) over
two threads
For stitch instructions, see pages 144
and 147.

Stitching the design
Two strands of Medicis crewel wool

have been used throughout.

Begin in any area you wish. It might be easiest to start at the top right-hand corner, 4–5cm (1½–2in) in from the corner, working from one block of colour to another. If you intend to use stitchery for part of the design, work this after completing the TENT stitch.

You can sew the whole design in TENT stitch (1) throughout. Alterna-tively, you can work certain areas of the design in stitchery to give an added dimension: see symbols on the chart for which stitch goes where, and refer to the colour photograph of the framed picture for the direction of the stitches.

The frills on the lady's dress and sleeves are sewn in horizontal SATIN stitch (3) and reversed TENT stitch (1) to give an unbroken line. The red seats are worked in vertical BRICK stitch (12) over two canvas threads.

Making up instructions

When the design has been sewn, the needlepoint may need to be stretched back into shape (see stretching in-structions on page 139). You may prefer to take your needlepoint to a professional picture framer who will also stretch it for you.

PIERROT

Pierrot first appeared in commedia dell'arte in the sixteenth century. One of our favourite subjects, he sits, sensitive and wistful, appealing and a little melancholy. He is shown here alone, isolated within a complex border, the stream of life flowing at his feet. This is an interesting design to work because of the multi-textured stitches used.

Finished size of design
23×27cm (9×10¾in)

Yarns
Appleton's crewel wool

751 pink 1 skein	**931** marron 2 skeins	**206** terracotta 1 skein
141 dull pink 2 skeins	**933** mauve 2 skeins	**181** beige 1 skein
		521 green 2 skeins

A 877
pale peach
3 skeins

B 883
heather
4 skeins

Anchor stranded cotton

C 869
lilac
5 skeins

01
white
3 skeins

D 892
peach
4 skeins

Canvas
18-gauge white mono de luxe
Size: 33×38cm (13×15in)

Other materials
Tapestry needle, size 22
Ruler or tape measure
Masking tape for binding the canvas
Sharp scissors for cutting the canvas
Embroidery scissors
Sharp HB pencil or fine permanent
   marker in a suitable colour
Eraser

Marking the canvas
Cut the canvas to size and bind the edges with masking tape. Mark out the canvas using an HB pencil or permanent marker in a pale shade. The chart has been drawn to scale. Each square of the graph represents one hole of the canvas and the lines represent the threads.

Count the squares and then draw the horizontal and vertical lines on the thread of the canvas. The diagonal lines should follow either the 'under' or 'over' threads of the canvas (see *figs. 1* and *2* on page 39). Double-check that you have marked the canvas accurately. If you have made a mistake, the pattern will not work out.

Refer to the colour picture and the chart and trace the Pierrot and butterfly from page 156 on to the canvas, taking care with their positioning. Erase the lines that go through the Pierrot and butterfly.

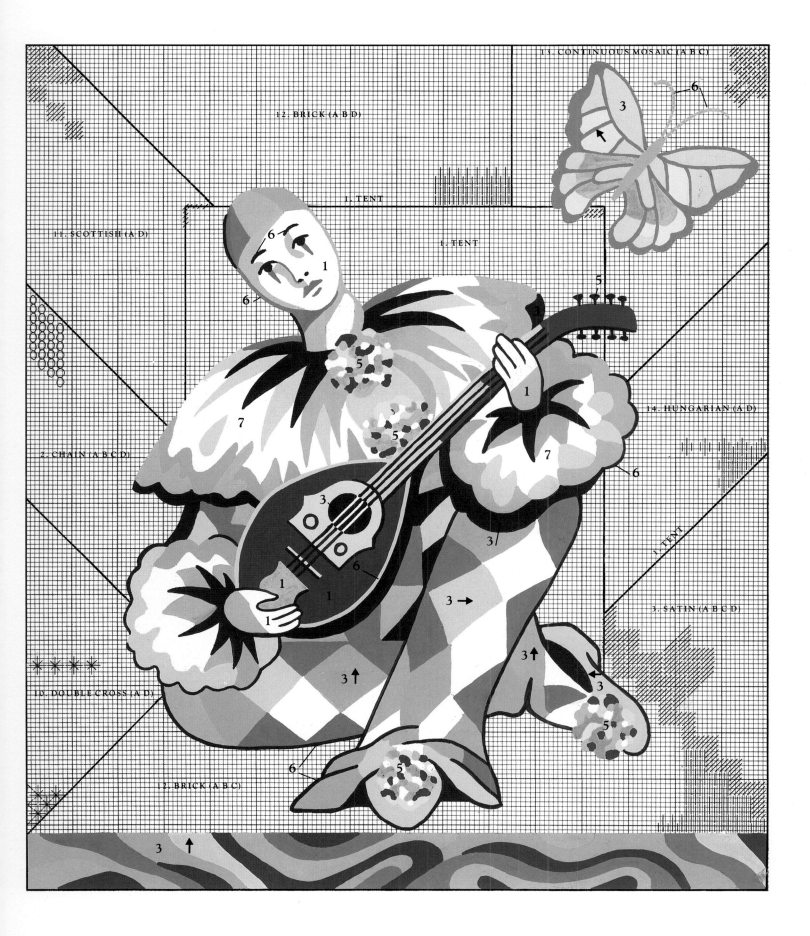

Stitches used
TENT and reversed TENT stitch (1)
CHAIN stitch (2)
SATIN stitch (3)
FRENCH KNOTS (5)
SPLIT BACK stitch (6)
LONG AND SHORT stitch (7)
DOUBLE CROSS stitch (10)
SCOTTISH stitch (11)
BRICK stitch (12)
CONTINUOUS MOSAIC stitch (13)
HUNGARIAN stitch (14)
For stitch instructions, see pages 144–7.

Stitching the design
Two strands of crewel wool have been used throughout with the exception of the features on the Pierrot's face, the outlining of the face and hands, and the strings on the mandolin, where one strand has been used. The whole thread of stranded cotton has been used (six strands).

For the position, colour and direction of the stitches refer to the chart and the photograph of the made-up Pierrot. The arrows on the SATIN stitch areas (3) show the direction. It may be necessary to use compensating stitches from time to time. On the stitchery background, when working a stitch in alternate colours, a beginner may find it easier to finish at the end of the first row and re-thread the needle in the other colour when beginning the next row.

White stranded cotton is used in the costume and on the Pierrot's face and hands. Lilac and peach stranded cotton are used on the pompons and in the background stitchery. Lilac stranded cotton is also used for dividing the stitch areas. Crewel wool is used everywhere else.

Begin by working the Pierrot, followed by the butterfly, then the water at the bottom and finally the stitchery background.

Pierrot and butterfly
The Pierrot's face, neck and hands are worked in TENT stitch (1) edged in SPLIT BACK stitch (6); his features are also worked in SPLIT BACK stitch (6). His costume is in vertical and horizontal SATIN stitch (3) edged in SPLIT BACK stitch (6). The ruff and the cuffs are in LONG AND SHORT stitch (7) edged in SPLIT BACK stitch (6) and SATIN stitch (3). The pompons on his ruff and on his shoes are in FRENCH KNOTS (5); the shoes are in SATIN stitch (3). The mandolin is in TENT stitch (1), SATIN stitch (3) and SPLIT BACK stitch (6). The butterfly is in SATIN stitch (3) and SPLIT BACK stitch (6). The water at the bottom is stitched in vertical SATIN stitch (3).

Stitchery background
Divide each stitch area with lilac TENT stitch (1) in stranded cotton on the lines marked on the canvas. On the diagonal lines on the left side of the border we have reversed the direction of the TENT stitch (1) to give an unbroken line. The stepped line edging the bargello pattern at the bottom of the design has *not* been edged in TENT stitch (1).

Working clockwise, stitch each area, starting with CONTINUOUS MOSAIC stitch (13) and ending with BRICK stitch (12). Begin as shown on the diagram. Fill in with compensating stitches around the Pierrot wherever necessary. Finally sew the 'sky' in heather crewel wool in TENT stitch (1).

Making up instructions.
When the design has been sewn, the needlepoint may need to be stretched back into shape (see stretching instructions on page 139). You may prefer to take your needlepoint to a professional picture framer who will also stretch it for you.

Left: At a palazzo watergate entrance, an arrangement of iron and stone that enhances the delicacy of the Pierrot picture.

Venice has acted as Muse for countless poets over the centuries. Anticipating Robert Browning, Byron said of Venice: 'Here have I pitched my staff, here do I purpose to reside for the remainder of my life.'

> *I stood in Venice, on the Bridge of Sighs;*
> *A palace and a prison on each hand:*
> *I saw from out the wave her structures rise*
> *As from the stroke of the enchanter's wand:*
> *A thousand years their cloudy wings expand*
> *Around me, and a dying Glory smiles*
> *O'er the far times, when many a subject land*
> *Look'd to the winged Lion's marble piles,*
> *Where Venice sate in state, throned on her hundred isles!*

In Life, as well as Literature, his connection with the city is legendary and he is included here in the Carnival section because that was the world he inhabited – when the prolonged Carnival season ended, Byron's pleasures continued. One of the most documented features of his stay in Venice is his lack of interest in needlework – though doubtless when he swam home up the Grand Canal, his manservant who followed with clothes held aloft ensured that they included a monogrammed lace kerchief.

He described the agonies of one new intrigue with a statement that exposes much of Venice itself: 'I met her at the Masque, and when her mask is off I am as wise as ever.' The decay that bothered others, the skull inside the *Bautta*, suited his poet's temperament. Also, at the time he arrived, the Venetians' economy was becoming precarious and they were determinedly cultivating the enjoyment of the moment, which coincided with Byron's desire to make what he could of his race against middle age, to 'work the mine of my youth to the last veins of the ore and then . . . goodnight'.

Carnival caught Byron in its whirlwind – he submerged himself in the dissipations of Venetian life, and with his *gondolieri* procuring for him in the streets, became promiscuous with an enthusiasm unprecedented even for him. The previous year it was said that Byron 'intensely desired to be exceedingly miserable', but Shelley wrote of him that since arriving in Venice, he had 'changed into the liveliest and happiest looking man I ever met'.

His first mistress in Venice was Marianna Segati, the wife of a draper, who was his landlady in the Frezzeria, near Piazza di San Marco. She was superseded by Margarita Cogni, the Fornarina (baker's wife) who joined his outrageous menagerie of servants, guests and animals at Palazzo Mocenigo (the damp ground floor was taken up with his carriages, a wolf, a fox, dogs, birds and monkeys). The Fornarina was the most tempestuous of his liaisons in Venice, which for him was only one of her qualities: she was twenty-two and being unable either to read or to write could not plague him with letters, and also, not having had children, had not fallen victim to our fate as women by becoming 'relaxed and doughy and lumpity a short time after breeding'. She installed herself as

housekeeper at Palazzo Mocenigo, terrified the staff into sub-mission and cut the bills to less than half. Byron was paying £200 a year rent for the palace, and had spent £4,000 since his arrival just on women, so he enjoyed the economies the wonderful virago effected. One story he related, of her waiting for him outside the palace in a storm, creates a powerful picture:

> *the gondola put in peril – hats blown away, boats filling, oar lost, tumbling sea, thunder, rain in torrents, night coming and wind increasing. On our return, after a tight struggle, I found her on the open steps . . . with her great black eyes flashing through her tears and the long dark hair, which was streaming, drenched with rain . . . lightning flashing round her, with the waves rolling at her feet, made her look like Medea alighted from her chariot . . . Seeing me safe she did not wait to greet me but called out 'Ah! Dog of the Virgin, is this a time to go to the Lido?'*

Venice was rife with gossip of the English nobleman with the scandalous life-style. Although it was a period of great creative excitement for Byron, the mumming and the masked balls of Carnival were wearing, and the debauchery of 'three or four up-all-nights' in quick succession now brought bloated physical deterioration. The knuckles of his hands were 'lost in fat' (surely not doughy and lumpity, L.B.?) and the headshaking of his doctors made him reform his wild household at Palazzo Mocenigo. The Fornarina was making greater and greater demands upon him and became 'quite ungovernable' and when told to leave the Palazzo, she snatched a knife from the table and threw herself into the canal. Byron was no sympathizer with female suicides and resuscitated her calmly. He was soon to meet his last great attachment, Teresa Guiccioli, but in the meantime the door between youth and middle age closed and brought with it an emptiness. The Carnival was over.

And incidentally, the Fornarina's nephew had an embroidered waistcoat.

Overleaf: Still Life – palazzo watergate, a Gothic bench, umbrellas like two tangoing flamingoes, a football for Italian passion (caged in a shopping basket), abandoned carnival masks. The cushion shows the elements we associate with Carnival: masks, music, a domino. And stardust.

CARNIVAL

Many of the elements we associate with Carnival — masks, musical instruments, a domino, a lace fan — are all caught up in swirling ribbons and tassels, scrolls and stardust, in colours of Venetian walls and water, with metallic gold for highlights.

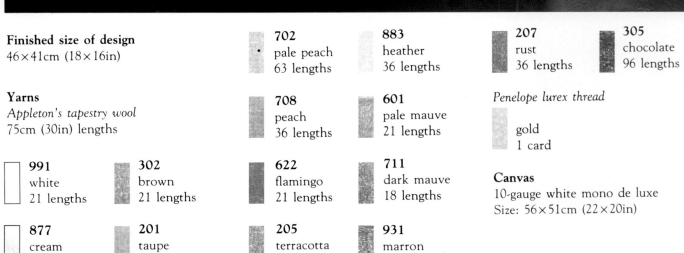

Finished size of design
46×41cm (18×16in)

Yarns
Appleton's tapestry wool
75cm (30in) lengths

991
white
21 lengths

877
cream
45 lengths

302
brown
21 lengths

201
taupe
45 lengths

702
pale peach
63 lengths

708
peach
36 lengths

622
flamingo
21 lengths

205
terracotta
48 lengths

883
heather
36 lengths

601
pale mauve
21 lengths

711
dark mauve
18 lengths

931
marron
60 lengths

207
rust
36 lengths

305
chocolate
96 lengths

Penelope lurex thread

gold
1 card

Canvas
10-gauge white mono de luxe
Size: 56×51cm (22×20in)

Other materials
Tapestry needle, size 18
Ruler or tape measure
Masking tape for binding the canvas
Sharp scissors for cutting the canvas
Embroidery scissors
Sharp HB pencil or fine permanent
   marker in a suitable colour
Eraser

Following the chart
Cut the canvas to size and bind the edges with masking tape. The design does not have to be marked out on the canvas; just follow the colour chart which is shown above. Remember that the squares of the chart represent the canvas intersections, not the holes. Each square represents one tent stitch.

The chart is divided up into units of 10 squares by 10 squares to make it easier to follow. Before beginning to stitch, it may be helpful to mark out your canvas in similar units of 10 squares by 10 squares with an HB pencil or permanent marker in a suitable colour. Also, we suggest marking the top of the canvas so that if you turn the canvas while you are stitching, you will still know where the top is.

The colours on the chart are shown stronger than the actual yarn colours to make them easier to see. The corresponding yarns are given in the colour key.

Stitches used
TENT stitch (1)
BACK stitch (4)
STEM stitch (8)
For stitch instructions, see pages 144 and 145.

Stitching the design
Use the whole thread of tapestry wool throughout. The gold lurex is worked double.

TENT stitch (1) is used throughout, except for the violin strings and the clef which are in STEM stitch (8), and the musical notes which are in BACK stitch (4).

Begin in any area you wish. It might be easiest to start at the top right-hand corner, 4–5cm (1½–2in) in from the corner, working from one block of colour to another.

Making up instructions
When the design has been sewn, the needlepoint may need to be stretched back into shape (see stretching instructions on page 139). Then make it up into a cushion of your choice as shown on pages 140–1.

MANDOLIN AND MASK
and VENETIAN BRIDGES

Two miniature pictures in the old rose, terracotta and muted tones of the ancient city show the architectural detail of stonework, wrought iron and balustrading with the masks and mandolin associated with Carnival. The pictures are worked mainly in subtle crewel wool shades in tent stitch, using metallic gold for highlights.

Finished size of each design
15.5×22cm (6×8½in)

Canvas
For each design:
18-gauge white mono de luxe
Size: 26×32cm (10×12½in)

Other materials
Tapestry needle, size 22
Ruler or tape measure
Masking tape for binding the canvas
Sharp scissors for cutting the canvas
Embroidery scissors
Sharp HB pencil or fine permanent
    marker in a suitable colour
Eraser

Following the charts
These two designs are worked in the same way unless otherwise indicated.

Cut the canvas to size and bind the edges with masking tape. The design does not have to be marked out on the canvas; just follow the colour charts on pages 114 and 115. Remember that the squares represent the canvas intersections, not the holes. Each square represents one tent stitch.

The charts are divided up into units of 10 squares by 10 squares to make them easier to follow. Before beginning to stitch, it may be helpful to mark out your canvas in similar units of 10 squares by 10 squares with an HB pencil or a permanent marker in a suitable colour. Also, we suggest marking the top of the canvas so that if you turn the canvas while stitching, you will still know where the top is.

The colours on the charts are shown stronger than the actual yarn colours to make them easier to see. The corresponding yarns are given in the colour keys.

Stitches used
For Mandolin and Mask design:
TENT stitch (1)
BACK stitch (4)
For Venetian Bridges design:
TENT stitch (1) is used throughout.

For stitch instructions, see pages 144 and 145.

Stitching the design
Two strands of crewel wool have been used throughout, except where gold is needed, when the whole thread is used singly.

Begin with TENT stitch (1) in any area you wish. It might be easiest to start at the top right-hand corner, 4–5cm (1½–2in) in from the corner, working from one block of colour to another. Finally, the gold areas on the mandolin and mask in the first design are worked in BACK stitch (4).

Making up instructions
When the designs have been sewn, they may need to be stretched back into shape (see stretching instructions on page 139). You may prefer to take your needlepoint to a professional picture framer who will also stretch it.

**For Mandolin
and Mask
design:**

Yarns
*Appleton's
crewel wool*

983
beige
2 skeins

202
mushroom
1 skein

142
pink
2 skeins

204
terracotta
2 skeins

226
plum
3 skeins

877
cream
2 skeins

*Penelope
lurex thread*

gold
1 card

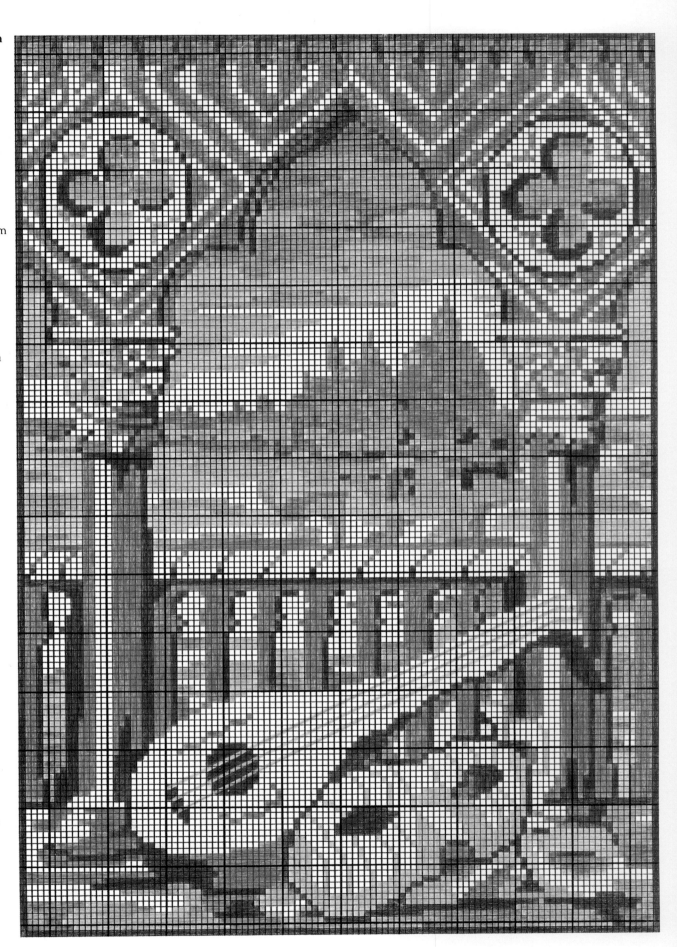

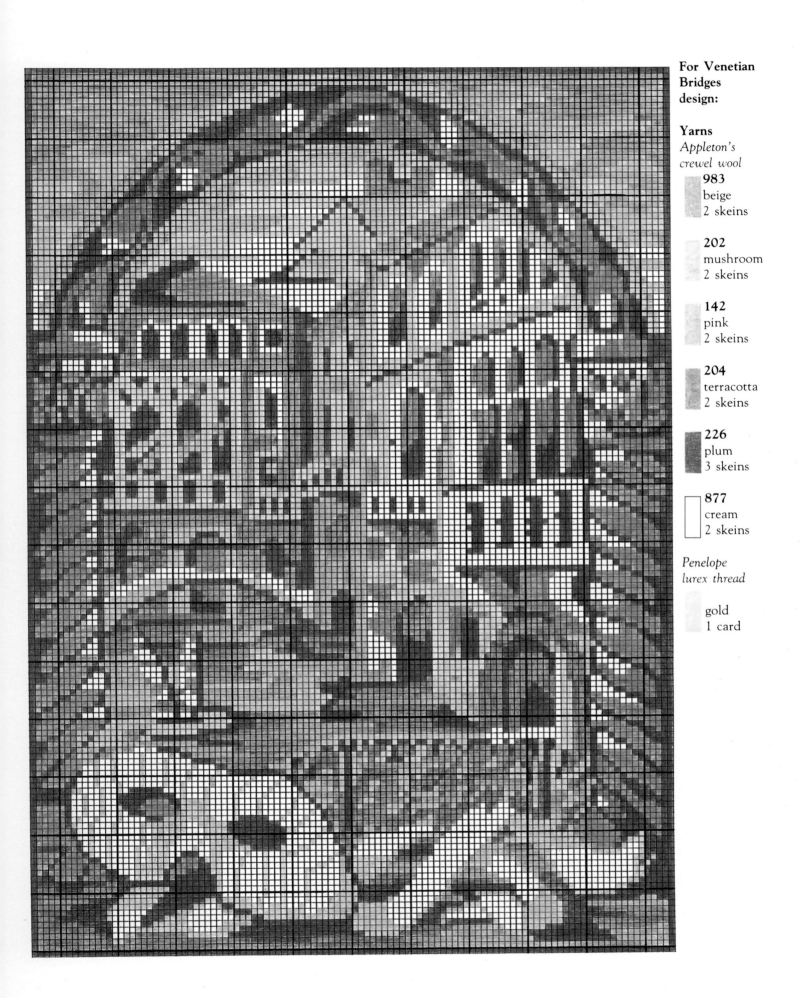

For Venetian Bridges design:

Yarns
Appleton's crewel wool

983
beige
2 skeins

202
mushroom
2 skeins

142
pink
2 skeins

204
terracotta
2 skeins

226
plum
3 skeins

877
cream
2 skeins

Penelope lurex thread

gold
1 card

CRAFTS AND

CHARACTERS

LACE

Lace is almost always something beautiful, a fantastical cobweb. It can be synonymous with a virginal lowering of lashes or a veiled seduction, an ostentatious froth of showmanship or a framework of purity on a baby's skin. The language of lace makes pictures: diaphanous, cascading, nostalgic, and above all ethereal. *Punto in aria* – stitches in air. And it is not a great stretch of imagination to look at the flowery Venetian Gothic architecture, the stone filigree work, the openness of the colonnades, the scalloped edges of Ca' d'Oro and notice the similarity to the collars, jabots, cuffs, baroque flounces, rococo roses and decorative spirals of lace as portrayed by the Venetian painters.

The design for our Lace project opposite was inspired by two nineteenth-century pieces. Both are made from multicoloured silks and we wanted to re-create the wonderful chiaroscuro effect of lace on a dark background. The obvious background colour to show off the creamy greens and peaches was black, but we wanted to suggest a feeling that was gentle and muted, so we used a grey cotton, which is firm and contrasts in texture with the wool of the lace, which is less structured, more fabric.

The origins of Venetian lace remain unresolved. What is known is that the work was done by anonymous women either at home, or in convents, remedial homes and hospitals, so there was no official guild to control and record. Perhaps the Government was afraid that it would be unable to control an all-female trade, or thought that the work done was so modest that it made a guild unnecessary. Not until the latter part of the fifteenth century are references made to lace, its uses and popularity. Venetian lace was in evidence at the coronation of Richard III in 1483; a Doge's wife founded a school; the aristocratic Venetian woman, it is believed, appreciated lace, its value as a skill and its use as ornament. There is also a lack of physical evidence: by its nature lace does not survive the centuries as does a piece of stone, and not until the sixteenth century did lace begin to appear on portraits.

The word lace comes from *lacis*, which can mean the art of making fishnets, and to us this confirms the only plausible explanation of the origin of lace. A sailor brought home to his sweetheart a gift of strange seaweed, given to him by mermaids. After he returned to sea, the girl consoled herself in her loneliness by copying the seaweed in whatever threads she had available: linen, silk and even her own hair. It is the most likely story for something of which dreams are spun.

Below: An example of Venetian lace, work of astonishing delicacy – 'stitches in air'.
Opposite: The needlepoint Lace cushion is based on fragments of lace from the nineteenth century, depicting multicoloured flowers and birds.

Paintings chart the fashion of lace, the shapes of collars, shawls, cuffs and ruffs, particularly in Pietro Longhi's portraits in Ca' Rezzonico. Baroque and rococo taste influenced clothing, lace became richer, a slavish race to luxury followed French and Spanish fashion, and laws had to be enforced curbing 'excesses'. The lace was made of cotton and linen, silk, wool, gold and silver yarns (and even, of course, hair), either by young orphaned girls or those 'gifted with beauty and lacking the means of making an honest living and close to being ruined forever'.

When the eighteenth-century decline came, with economic and artistic areas suffering, salvation for the lace industry came through a noblewoman, Adriana Marcello, who began a school in Burano with Paulo Fambri. Michelangelo Jesurum started his school in Pellestrina, at a time when nineteenth-century fashion demanded lace to be applied to *everything*, calling Pellestrina's lace 'a confusion of threads arranged with horrible taste and even more dreadful workmanship'. His first step was the founding of the Society for Venetian Lace Manufacture and he became a much needed father-figure in the resurgence of the lace industry . . . and the stories of child lacemakers' eyesight being so affected that they could only work for a few years? Tragically true.

The Jesurum shop on Rio della Canonica, on the 'other side' of the Bridge of Sighs, has some spectacular examples of old lace on view and newer lace to buy. There is also a marble bust outside in the courtyard of an ivy-trailed Signor Jesurum, who by all accounts was so loved, looking like a tax inspector sucking a lemon.

While lace experts universally credit Venice with the invention of needle lace and *punto in aria*, Venetian bobbin lace is glossed over as though it were of little importance, though it easily rivalled needle lace for beauty – imagine exquisite collars made with as many as 1,500 bobbins. In 1879 Paulo Fambri describes the bobbin lace technique as follows (it reads like an excerpt from *Lace Making for Masochists*):

> *The lacemaker is merely she whom the bobbins seek. To pursue them is to go mad . . . the work is an entwining of a greater or lesser number of threads depending on the difficulty of the design. This, you understand, cannot be done in mid-air. They (the threads) would dangle, despite being weighted by a plummet or bobbin at the free end, and at each brusque movement they would head off in a hundred directions, producing hopeless tangles and Gordian knots impossible to free except with scissors . . . To avoid this, the bobbin lacemaker seats herself rather comfortably in front of a stool, holding a full cylindrical or spherical sack in her ample arms . . . On this she places the strip with the pattern whose main points, 100, 200, 500 or more are indicated by as many pins, the predetermined points of numerous intersections . . . And it all consists of knowing, among the hundreds of ends, which two or more should be joined at that instant, then letting them go and moving on to others for which other unions are intended, and having put them in the right place, running with your eyes and hands to the third, fourth, thousandth combination, and having exhausted these, moving the pins for the next intersections according to the twists and turns of the dots and lines to be reproduced, even replacing the original bobbins with others when, by chance, they have to change the colours or their shading.*

An interesting footnote: at an exhibition in Rome in 1887, the prize in the Lace category was won by the San Clemente Women's Insane Asylum in Venice. Some of the women were from Pellestrina and lacemakers by profession. They could have been institutionalized for the reasons described above, but the formal reasons were either 'manias' or because of behaviour so peculiar as to be considered a madness: 'not wanting to do housework'. O Tempora, O Mores!

Venetian traditions continue today as always. Opposite: A scene that has not changed in centuries – Venice's equivalent of the Glorafilia ladies, mellowing in years, indulging in a little light industry as the ragù simmers indoors. One has just said to the other, 'Listen, Maria, I have a couple of needlepoint kits hidden in my bottom drawer. Shall we give this lacemaking a break?'

LACE

The cushion was inspired by nineteenth-century fragments of lace depicting birds and flowers in a rich pictorial way. These antique pieces were made from multicoloured silks, the colours changing to give the impression of a subtle play of light over the surface.

Finished size of design
29cm (11½in) square

Yarns
Appleton's tapestry wool
75cm (30in) lengths

691
pale green
54 lengths

877
cream
21 lengths

951
olive
36 lengths

203
terracotta
21 lengths

704
peach
72 lengths

987
pale grey
36 lengths

DMC coton perlé No.3
414
dark grey
7 skeins

Canvas
14-gauge white mono de luxe
Size: 39cm (15½in) square

Other materials
Tapestry needle, size 20
Ruler or tape measure
Masking tape for binding the canvas
Sharp scissors for cutting the canvas
Embroidery scissors
Sharp HB pencil or fine permanent
    marker in a suitable colour
Eraser

Following the chart
Cut the canvas to size and bind the edges with masking tape. The design does not have to be marked out on the canvas; just follow the colour chart opposite. Remember that the squares of the chart represent the canvas intersections, not the holes. Each square represents one tent stitch.

The chart is divided up into units of 10 squares by 10 squares to make it easier to follow. Before beginning to stitch, it may be helpful to mark out your canvas in similar units of 10 squares by 10 squares with an HB pencil or permanent marker in a suitable colour.

Also, we suggest marking the top of the canvas so that if you turn the canvas while you are stitching the design, you will still know where the top is.

The colours on the chart are shown stronger than the actual yarn colours to make them easier to see. The corresponding yarn shades and the lengths required are given in the colour key.

Stitches used
TENT stitch (1) is used throughout. For stitch instructions, see page 144.

Stitching the design
The whole thread is used throughout. Begin in any area you wish. It might be easiest to start at the top right-hand corner, 4–5cm (1½–2in) in from the corner, working from one block of colour to another.

Making up instructions
When the design has been sewn, the needlepoint may need to be stretched back into shape (see stretching instructions on page 139). Then make it up into a cushion of your choice as shown on pages 140–1.

GLASS

Images of glass are inseparable from Venice. The city is viewed through circular window panes in a distortion of stone and light reflected from water. Hundreds of shops sparkle with tiny rainbow glass creatures standing on spindly legs, glass strung into glittering fruit salad necklaces, mirrors, music boxes, ashtrays, cockerels and clowns, sea-horses and swans – far outnumbering the beautiful goblets and crystalline *objets* that hold themselves aloof from the tidal wave of souvenirs.

Glassmaking began on a large scale in Venice in the thirteenth century, when to avoid fire all glasshouses were transferred from the city to the island of Murano. Once on Murano, the glassmakers were virtually prisoners, so afraid was the Grand Council that the secrets would become known outside Venice, and so strict their control. There were clear groups of manufacturers – the *margaritai* is the one that interests us most, the makers of mosaic and *millefiori* beads; the *perlai* made large hollow beads; *cristallai* made glass for spectacles; *specchiai* made mirrors; *fioleri* made goblets and the *venditori* sold them all. The Renaissance gave the Venetian glass industry great impetus, establishing her as the centre for glassmaking. Venetians developed ways of colouring glass with additions of copper for fine green tints, and made glass to resemble agate and onyx. Many innovations have been Venetian: filigree glass, aventurine (the sparkling gold-dust glass), enamelling on glass.

As with recipes for dyeing and lacquering, not only is the result extraordinary, but so is the feat of finding the materials with

which to make that result. Glass requires soda-ash from sea plants for alkali, white pebbles from the River Ticino as silica, powdered marble or crushed sea-shells for lime . . .

The mosaic beads were introduced in the fifteenth century, imitations of the ancient Roman process. The making of these beads, almost 'spun' from threads of coloured glass, has many stages, sounding to us like the drawing, rolling, compressing and fusing that goes on with making Chinese noodles. These beads were exported to Portugal, Spain, Africa, even China and were used to trade for gold, ivory, silver, spices. They have been found in excavations as distant as Tibet and Peru.

Millefiori, thousand flowers, is the technique most commonly seen on Venetian beads and paperweights, as little sunbursts of colour, but the mosaic design we have used is more interesting for needlepoint – satisfying interlocking shapes. In the project overleaf you can see one panel of a three-panel envelope bag and in the main photograph opposite the same design has been worked on a larger gauge canvas with correspondingly thicker yarn and shaped appropriately for the tortoiseshell frame.

Above: Venetian beads – beautiful, unique, rainbow handfuls of history, heavy as stone.
Opposite: A bag adapted from the needlepoint design overleaf, inspired by the interlocking shapes of fifteenth-century 'mosaic' beads.

EVENING BAG

The interlocking shapes of this pattern can be seen on antique 'mosaic' glass beads of the fifteenth century, used in trade for gold, ivory and spices – they have been found in excavations as far distant as Tibet and Peru. We have used the design for a three-panel evening bag in stranded cotton and gold metallic thread, and its interesting shapes, rather like the jigsaw puzzle of a tortoise shell, could be adapted very successfully to different sizes and colours.

Finished size of design
When made up, the bag measures 21.5×14.5cm (8½×5¾in). The completed needlepoint with three design repeats measures 21.5×43.5cm (8½×17¼in) before folding.

Yarns
Anchor stranded cotton

387
stone
10 skeins

311
yellow
6 skeins

400
grey
8 skeins

851
peacock green
4 skeins

779
kingfisher
4 skeins

369
pale sienna
4 skeins

943
gold
6 skeins

349
dark sienna
10 skeins

Penelope lurex thread

gold
1 card

Canvas
18-gauge white mono de luxe
Size: 32×54cm (12½×21¼in)

Other materials
Tapestry needle, size 22
Ruler or tape measure

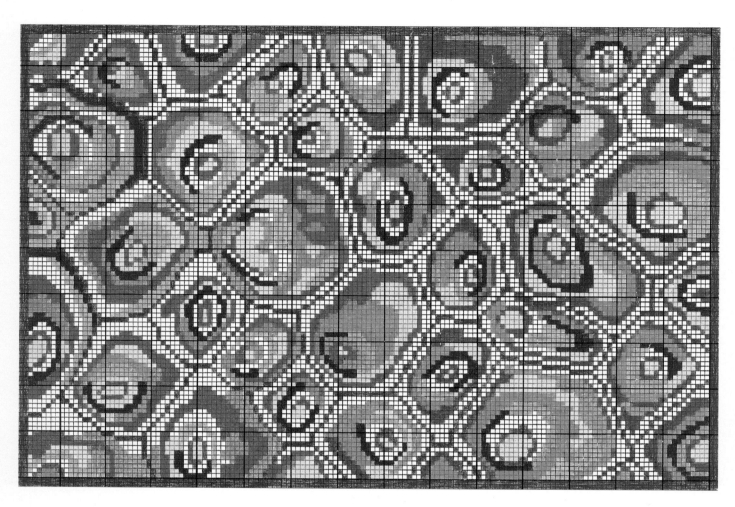

Masking tape for binding the canvas
Sharp scissors for cutting the canvas
Embroidery scissors
Sharp HB pencil or fine permanent
   marker in a suitable colour
Eraser

Following the chart

Cut the canvas to size and bind the
edges with masking tape. The design
does not have to be marked out on
the canvas; just follow the colour
chart above. It should be repeated
twice more for the evening bag (see
diagram, right). Remember that the
squares represent the canvas inter-
sections, not the holes. Each square
represents one tent stitch.

The chart is divided up into units
of 10 squares by 10 squares to make
it easier to follow. Before beginning
to stitch, it may be helpful to mark
out your canvas in similar units of
10 squares by 10 squares with an
HB pencil or permanent marker in
a suitable colour. Also, we suggest
marking the top of the canvas so that

if you turn it while stitching, you will
know where the top is.

The colours on the chart are
shown stronger than the actual yarn
colours to make them easier to see.

```
┌─────────────────┐
│                 │
│     REPEAT      │
│                 │
├─────────────────┤
│                 │
│     REPEAT      │
│                 │
├─────────────────┤
│                 │
│  AREA OF CHART  │  14.5cm
│                 │  (5¾in)
└─────────────────┘
     21.5cm (8½in)
```

The corresponding yarns are given in
the colour key.

Stitches used

TENT stitch (1) is used throughout.
For stitch instructions, see page 144.

Stitching the design

Use six strands (the whole thread) of
stranded cotton and one strand of
gold thread. Begin in any area you
wish. It might be easiest to start at
the top right-hand corner, 4–5cm
(1½–2in) in from the corner, working
from one block of colour to another.

Making up instructions

When the design has been sewn, the
needlepoint may need to be stretched
back into shape (see stretching instructions on page 139). Then make
it up into an evening bag as shown
on page 142.

MARBLING

Marbling paper began in France in the seventeenth century, was adopted by Florence and is now one of the traditional crafts of Venice. We walk quickly past the razzmatazz of the new marblers, and the heart lifts to find in a sombre street tiny shops where the floating paint is lovingly stroked with brushes, scribes, combs into kaleidoscope swirls, and the paper lowered on to it, letting the miraculous whirlpool designs appear. As with other special crafts, the recipes are secret, the ingredients – the leaves for the pigments to be used – coming from far-flung places. At Legatoria Piazzesi our eyes move around each sheet, trying to rest, finally stopping on a satisfyingly compli-cated piece of green and gold, that then links to a mauve ripple, and then a tidal wave of pink, fuchsia and maroon, and ebbs and flows across into cinnamon and coffee, umber and flame. We are children in a sweetshop and we want them all.

Choosing marbled paper for needlepoint designs was no easy matter. We drew each sheet from the stacks with the reverence of handling ancient manuscripts. Each possessed qualities the previous had not. Golds, look at these golds. No, not serene enough, look how these greens go from cold to hot. One has the calm marbling of stone, another is reminiscent of a Turkish market. We buy many, which Fabia Bos rolls in a tube. Only two are used for the designs, the rest pinned on the studio wall, just because they are so beautiful. A curiosity: the people who painted, stitched and charted these designs independently said the same thing – the patterning made them feel happy. Do the shapes imitate alphawaves, making the brain smile via the dazzled eye? Even assembling the colours was a delight – dozens of flowing possible choices star-scattered on the carpet.

LACQUERED AND GILDED FRAMES

In Venice you cross a bridge, enter *campielli*, and are beckoned by an unpainted doorway into gloom, certain that some treasure will be inside – maybe someone carving, or upholster-ing with nails in his mouth, the same dust settled on him that covers the pieces in the shop, none of which seem to be finished. Enter Campo Manin across Ponte de la Cortesia and a tiny emporium crouches just by the bridge. The door is open, the hallway and workroom are a balancing act of furniture and frames and decorated surfaces. Move slowly and hold your breath, lest one knock should make the contents topple like a house of cards. There is an unfamiliar smell: twenty-five years of varnish perhaps, sweet and strong. This is Barutti's. Barutti Senior founded the business – a musician, painter, sculptor, who produced six daughters and one son, Alfredo. Alfredo in turn has produced five sons, all of whom are musicians. There are no apprentices and Barutti's will die with him. He calls himself *L' Indorador e Lacador* – gilder and lacquerer, and what he makes are exquisite lacquer frames, as they have been made in Venice since the Middle Ages.

He developed the techniques passed on first by his father, then by a master. The pattern is incised on wood rubbed smooth with rabbit hide. The recipes for the lacquers read like Macbeth's witches' brew: oxidized pigment from cave ceilings ground with the white of egg, Indian resin, alcohol, ear of bat, gizzard of toad . . . horse fat is superior to pig fat for allowing the polishing bone to slide without ripping the gold leaf. He carves curves in antique wood and has brought generations of artisan framing to a fine art. The frames are unlike anything we've seen and are astonishingly beautiful.

We were curious to see if we could imitate one of his frames two-dimensionally, letting the multiple gold tones of silk make the hills and valleys of the raised work. The result has a beautiful *trompe-l'œil* effect. The Barutti design on page 136 could be enlarged for a magnificent border to a painting, or reduced and worked on small-gauge canvas to frame a miniature. Either way, we love the proportion of frame to subject and have used an antique mirror in the centre that does not detract from the needlepoint. Looking critically at what appears to be an all-gold lacquer frame with some highlights and shadows suddenly produces many colours, green golds, brown golds, dull golds, gold reflecting its surroundings and mirroring back other shining shades. His frames take a long time to complete, sometimes fifteen different stages of gilding. To work the needlepoint would take an appropriately long time too.

He reminisces: his father insisted he learn the trade formally, and when he first started working with his *maestro* he was eleven years old and earned one lira a week. After a while he earned five lire a week, which he was given as a silver coin, with instructions to buy a shirt and shoes. At fourteen, instead of more pay, his master let him go to school for a few hours. The story is charming, perhaps with a little embellishment for his rapt audience, though we do know that there was a song at the time where to be rich meant having a thousand lire. Really? we ask. '*Certo!*' he insists. Certainly!

* * *

As in every ancient city, there are wonderful characters in Venice, who so personify its traditions. One can only hope that future generations will provide something similar. The first shop to receive a licence in Venice was started by Rina Zennaro's grandfather, a woodworker. In 1901 the Government decided all shops had to join a commercial body and grand-pappa Zennaro received No. 1 licence. That sector of Venice, in the San Marco section, was willed to two brothers, with the codicil that if they tried to sell any piece of the property they would forfeit the other benefits, and this legacy has gone down through the generations.

At twenty, Rina was not married, and as with other Venetian unfortunates, she donned black. Suddenly at sixty, she realized that life had something to offer and began living – she is now in her eighties and having a wonderful time. You can pass her shop after closing at night and see her with friends, talking and laughing in a glowing cameo among the ashy carvings and furniture.

But try to buy anything in her shop? No. Oh, no, that has a little bit missing and she wouldn't sell it imperfect, that carving is in terrible condition, that picture needs restoration, the screen is not for sale, just because . . . There is only one piece left from her grandfather's woodwork, a thin wooden panel with his signature, so these other pieces are not of

sentimental value for that reason. Perhaps they are collected and loved like the children she never had. She talks of beginning to make her 'bottom drawer' from the age of eight or nine, and told us of a lady she knew, also unmarried, who died at ninety-two and left a chest full of stunning fabrics, underclothes and linens, infinitesimal pleats joined with lace. In her elegant poetical Italian she described how life and laundry used to be: you'd need one woman to put the linens to 'soak'; two days later the water would be changed, the garments handwashed and precisely hung out without creases; the following day a special woman would come in only to iron the linen. As servants became more expensive, less linen taking so many days to launder was used. She remembers using a 'form' to slip into her still-wet stockings to dry them flat with a 'seam', and still uses a similar form for gloves.

Opposite: An example of the glorious marbled paper that inspired our cushion overleaf.
Above: Alfredo Barutti – gilder, lacquerer and great character of Venice, who describes his work with a passion, aware that the techniques of his craft will die out – he has no apprentice, and his sons will not follow in his footsteps.

MARBLED CUSHION

The beautiful craft of paper marbling, adopted by the Venetians, suggested the design for this cushion. The glorious colours come from leaf pigments and 'secret ingredients', which are combed and brushed into spirals of colour and then transferred miraculously on to paper, where they ebb and flow in extraordinary combinations of tones. The canvas is worked entirely in tent stitch in stranded cotton and gold metallic thread.

Finished size of design
31cm (12in) square

Yarns
Anchor stranded cotton

846 dark olive 6 skeins		**849** turquoise 2 skeins	
859 mid ash green 4 skeins		**870** heather 1 skein	
8581 grey green 3 skeins		**103** orchid 2 skeins	
844 olive 4 skeins		**969** pink 2 skeins	
213 eau de nil 4 skeins		**970** mauve 2 skeins	
842 grass 3 skeins		**897** burgundy 2 skeins	
379 tobacco 2 skeins		**339** rust 1 skein	
872 purple 1 skein		**390** ecru 3 skeins	
883 terracotta 3 skeins			

Astrella metallic thread

gold
7 skeins

Canvas
14-gauge white mono de luxe
Size: 41cm (16in) square

Other materials
Tapestry needle, size 20
Ruler or tape measure
Masking tape for binding the canvas
Sharp scissors for cutting the canvas
Embroidery scissors
Sharp HB pencil or fine permanent
    marker in a suitable colour
Eraser

Following the chart
Cut the canvas to size and bind the edges with masking tape. The design does not have to be marked out on the canvas; just follow the colour chart opposite. Remember that the squares represent the canvas intersections, not the holes. Each square represents one tent stitch.

The chart is divided up into units of 10 squares by 10 squares to make it easier to follow. Before beginning to stitch, it may be helpful to mark out your canvas in similar units of 10 squares by 10 squares with an HB pencil or permanent marker in a suitable colour. Also, we suggest marking the top of the canvas so that if you turn the canvas while stitching, you will still know where the top is.

The colours on the chart are shown stronger than the actual yarn colours to make them easier to see. The corresponding yarns are given in the colour key.

Stitches used
TENT stitch (1) is used throughout. For stitch instructions, see page 144.

Stitching the design
Use six strands (the whole thread) of stranded cotton and two strands of gold thread.

Begin in any area you wish. It might be easiest to start at the top right-hand corner, 4–5cm (1½–2in) in from the corner, working from one block of colour to another.

Making up instructions
When the design has been sewn, the needlepoint may need to be stretched back into shape (see stretching instructions on page 139). Then make it up into a cushion of your choice as shown on pages 140–1.

THE BARUTTI FRAME

This project was inspired by the gilded and lacquered frames which have been made in Venice since the Middle Ages. We have imitated on canvas the incised and gold-leafed wood, using tones of gold cotton and metal thread to give a fascinating trompe-l'œil effect.

Previous page: The Barutti frame, incognito.

Finished size of design
28.5cm (11¼in) square

Yarns
Anchor stranded cotton

386 lemon 3 skeins		**901** ginger 10 skeins	
301 pale yellow 6 skeins		**375** brown 3 skeins	
891 yellow ochre 10 skeins			

Penelope lurex thread

gold
2 cards

Canvas
18-gauge white mono de luxe
Size: 38.5cm (15¼in) square

Other materials
Tapestry needle, size 22
Ruler or tape measure
Masking tape for binding the canvas
Sharp scissors for cutting the canvas
Embroidery scissors
Sharp HB pencil or fine permanent
   marker in a suitable colour
Eraser

Following the chart
Cut the canvas to size and bind the edges with masking tape. The design does not have to be marked out on the canvas; just follow the colour chart opposite. Remember that the squares of the chart represent the canvas intersections, not the holes. Each square represents one tent stitch.

The chart is divided up into units of 10 squares by 10 squares to make it easier to follow. Before beginning to stitch, it may be helpful to mark out your canvas in similar units of 10 squares by 10 squares with an HB pencil or permanent marker in a suitable colour. Also, we suggest marking the top of your canvas so that if you turn the canvas while stitching, you will still know where the top is.

The colours on the chart are shown stronger than the actual yarn colours to make them easier to see. The corresponding yarn shades and the number of skeins required are given in the colour key.

Stitches used

TENT stitch (1)
SATIN stitch (3)
For stitch instructions, see page 144.

Stitching the design

Use the whole thread of gold lurex
and six strands (the whole thread) of
stranded cotton.

Begin in any area you wish. It
might be easiest to start at the top
right-hand corner, 4–5cm (1½–2in)
in from the corner, working from one
block of colour to another.

Most of the design is worked in
TENT stitch (1), except for the outer
and inner borders which are in
SATIN stitch (3). For the position of
the stitches refer to the colour chart
and the photograph of the made-up
frame. The arrows indicate the direction of the SATIN stitch.

Making up instructions

When the design has been sewn, the
needlepoint may need to be stretched
back into shape (see stretching instructions on page 139). Then make
it up into a mirror or photo frame as
shown on page 143.

GENERAL INFORMATION

MARKING THE CANVAS

☐ Always leave a border of at least 5cm (2in) of unstitched canvas all around the edges of the design for stretching purposes.

☐ When marking out a canvas into squares of 10 threads by 10 threads, you should use a permanent marker, an HB pencil or a water-erasable marking pen.

☐ To trace a design through on to canvas, place the canvas on top of the drawing and mark the outline with a permanent marker, an HB pencil or a water-erasable marking pen.

The trace patterns in this book have been given a heavy outline so that you can trace directly from the page if you wish, but if you don't want to risk spoiling the book, draw the design on to tracing paper first, using a black marker.

A design can also be painted on to canvas in oil or acrylic paint, using a soft fine brush. Ensure that whatever medium you use is waterproof as it would be disastrous if the colour ran when the work was dampened for stretching.

☐ When marking out a design on linen, use a water-erasable marking pen or an embroidery transfer pencil.

PLANNING A STITCHING SEQUENCE

☐ When working from a chart, try to work from the top right-hand corner from one block of colour to another.

☐ We suggest you use the basket-weave method on a large area of tent stitch as it does not put a strain on the canvas and a more even tension is achieved.

☐ When working a design using stitchery, it is advisable to work the outlining first, then the design and finally the background, but there are no hard-and-fast rules. Use compensating stitches (small filling-in stitches) where necessary.

☐ White yarn should be left to the end for an obvious reason – to keep it clean. Don't let the ends of other colours get caught into the stitches.

WORKING METHODS

☐ We suggest that you use a frame when stitching, but this is a personal choice. There is no question that the finish is better and a more even tension is achieved, but if you are more comfortable working without a frame, that is fine.

☐ Some people need a thimble, and at some point in your needlepoint career you may well need a seam unpicker!

☐ Cut your tapestry wool into lengths of approximately 75cm (30in); cut stranded cotton, coton perlé, gold thread and crewel wool into 38–50cm (15–20in) lengths.

☐ To begin, knot the wool temporarily on the front of the canvas about 2.5cm (1in) from where you want to start, in the direction in which you will be working. As you work your canvas, the stitches on the back will anchor the 2.5cm (1in) thread. When you reach the knot, cut it off and the thread should be quite secure. When you re-thread your needle to continue sewing the same area, there is no need to knot the wool; simply run the needle through the work on the underside. And to finish, do the same in reverse.

☐ Keep the back tidy – there are two simple reasons for this. Firstly, having lots of ends hanging at the back can eventually make it difficult to get your needle through the canvas. Secondly, the work will lie flatter when it is made up. So cut your threads short when you have anchored them.

AND FINALLY

☐ When framing a needlepoint picture, we never use glass. Nor would we put glass on an oil painting. These deserve to be enjoyed as textured and interesting pieces, not flattened and diminished behind glass.

☐ To keep needlepoint pictures clean, just flick over with a feather duster. Ideally, needlepoint should not be in a smoky atmosphere – and after all, stitching is an excellent way of cutting down on smoking.

☐ Needlepoint can be Scotch-Guarded and we strongly recommend that you do not wash it. Take it to a good dry cleaner's instead. Embroideries can be washed gently by hand, using cool water and a mild detergent.

ADAPTING CHARTS AND ARTWORK

When following a chart, you can easily change the gauge of canvas you choose. If you decide on 10-gauge canvas (canvas with 10 holes to the inch) when we have suggested 18-gauge canvas (canvas with 18 holes to the inch), remember that the design will be almost twice the size. It is important, too, to change the yarn to a more suitable thickness, and the needle size also. Similarly, if we suggest 10-gauge canvas and you use 18-gauge canvas, the finished needlepoint will be almost half the size.

An example of this is the Purple Brocade project on page 26. We have shown the same design worked on 7-gauge canvas as a bolster and on 14-gauge canvas as a cushion.

The chart on the opposite page will help if you decide to change the dimensions of a project.

Artwork can be enlarged or reduced in size at your local photocopy shop. Likewise, if you are adapting a photograph, do a tracing of it first and have the tracing enlarged or reduced. Then transfer the design on to your canvas as described in Marking the Canvas (above).

CANVAS/YARN/NEEDLE CHART

Single thread canvas (mono)	Appleton's tapestry wool in skeins or 25gr hanks* Anchor tapisserie wool in skeins	Appleton's crewel wool in skeins or 25gr hanks DMC Medicis crewel wool	DMC coton perlé Nos. 3 & 5 in skeins	Anchor stranded cotton in skeins (6 strands per thread)	Size of tapestry needle
10 holes to the inch (4 per cm)	1 thread for tent stitch (not stitchery)	4/5 threads depending on size of stitch		9/12 strands	18
14 holes to the inch (5 per cm)	1 thread	3 threads	No. 3 1 thread	6/9 strands	20
16 holes to the inch (6 per cm)		2/3 threads depending on size of stitch	No. 5 1/2 threads No. 3 1 thread	6 strands	22
18 holes to the inch (7 per cm)		2 threads	No. 5 1 thread	4/6 strands	22

* The formula is that two 75cm (30in) lengths of tapestry wool will cover 6.25 sq cm (1 sq in) in tent stitch. Therefore one 25gr hank [72×75cm (30in) lengths] will cover approximately 225 sq cm (36 sq in).

FINISHING AND MAKING UP

Many needlepointers feel experienced enough to stretch and make up their needlework designs into cushions, bags, stool tops and a variety of other items, but we always feel that a needlepoint picture should be framed by a professional who has particular experience at stretching and framing needlepoint.

If you would like to stretch your own needlepoint before making up, use the following method.

Stretching

Materials

Blotting paper
Clean flat board
Tacks, staples or drawing pins

The needlepoint must be 'square' before framing or making into a cushion, bag, stool top etc. If it is out of square, lightly damp or spray it and leave for a few minutes to soften the canvas. Gently pull square and then pin out, right side down, on to blotting paper on a clean flat board. Use tacks, staples or drawing pins and pin outside the sewn surface. Do not strain the canvas too tightly or the needlepoint will dry with a scalloped edge.

When the needlepoint is thoroughly dry (this may take two to three days), remove it from the board.

Making cushions

Instructions are given on pages 140–1 for making your needlepoint into a variety of cushion styles. Firm cotton, chintz, brocade and moiré are all easy fabrics to work with for the cushion backing. Medium-weight velvet also makes an attractive backing but is a little more difficult for beginners to handle. We don't recommend upholstery velvet, which is very thick.

Ready-made cushion pads can be bought in various sizes. For a flat effect, use a pad the same size as the needlepoint cover. For a plumper cushion, use a pad 5cm (2in) larger than the cover. Boxed cushions should have a pad with a gusset. Ease the pad into the cushion cover gently to avoid putting any strain on the zip, pushing it carefully into the corners to fill them out.

CUSHION WITH TWISTED CORD TRIM

Materials

0.5m (⅝yd) fabric 122cm (48in) wide or remnant slightly larger than cushion size
Zip 8cm (3in) shorter than height of finished cushion
Twisted cord 10cm (4in) longer than the measurement around the cushion
Pins
Clear adhesive tape

1. Stretch the needlepoint back to its original shape and cut away any excess canvas, leaving 1.2cm (½in) of unsewn canvas for turning.
2. Cut out the cushion back to the same size as the canvas, adding 5cm (2in) to the width measurement for the zip seam. Fold the fabric in half from side to side and cut along the crease to form the zip opening.
3. At each end of the zip opening, stitch a 5cm (2in) seam, taking 2.5cm (1in) turnings. Press seam open. Sew in the zip (*fig.1*). Remember to leave it open to turn the cushion through.

fig. 1

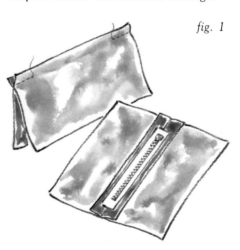

4. Tack or pin the fabric to the needlepoint right sides together. Machine around the edge of the needlepoint, leaving a 2.5cm (1in) opening at the bottom. Double stitch or overlock the seams. Turn the cushion to the right side through the zip opening.
5. Sew on the cord by hand starting from the opening at the bottom and leaving a small 'tail' (*fig.2*). (Before cutting the cord, wrap the ends with

fig. 2

adhesive tape to prevent them from fraying.) Join the cord by weaving the ends together and securing with a few stitches. Wrap the join with adhesive tape before cutting away any excess cord. Tuck the ends into the opening and neaten by sewing in.

* * *

CUSHION WITH NEEDLEPOINT PANEL

Materials

0.5m (⅝yd) fabric 122cm (48in) wide
Zip 8cm (3in) shorter than height of finished cushion
Twisted cord 10cm (4in) longer than measurement around cushion and panel seams
Pins
Clear adhesive tape

1. Stretch the needlepoint back to its original shape and cut away any excess canvas, leaving 1.2cm (½in) of unsewn canvas for turning.
2. Cut two pieces of fabric for the side panels to the same length as the needlepoint and as wide as you like, plus turnings. On the Yellow Panel project on page 18 the finished length of each side panel is 28.5cm (11¼in) and the width 10cm (4in).
3. Cut out the fabric for the cushion backing to measure as follows: the same length as the side panels (including turnings) × the two panel widths plus the width of the needlepoint in the centre (plus turnings) and adding 5cm (2in) for the zip allowance.
4. Fold the backing in half from side to side and cut along the crease. This is for the zip opening. Sew in the zip as for the cushion with the twisted cord trim (left), taking 2.5cm (1in) turnings.

5. Tack or pin the panels into place and machine close to the finished needlepoint. Sew cord along each seamline.

6. Tack cushion back to cushion front right sides together. Machine around the edge, leaving a 2.5cm (1in) opening at the bottom. Double stitch or overlock the seams. Turn the cushion to the right side through the zip opening.
7. Sew cord around the edge as for the cushion with the twisted cord trim, starting from the opening at the bottom and leaving a small tail. (Before cutting the cord, wrap the ends with adhesive tape to prevent them from fraying.) Join the cord by weaving the ends together and securing with a few stitches. Wrap the join with adhesive tape before cutting away any excess cord. Tuck the ends into the opening and neaten by sewing in.

* * *

CUSHION WITH MITRED FABRIC BORDER

Materials

0.5m (⅝yd) fabric 122cm (48in) wide
Zip 8cm (3in) shorter than height of finished cushion
Piping cord No.3 to fit around the inside and outside edges of the border
Pins

1. Stretch the needlepoint back to its original shape and cut away any excess canvas, leaving 1.2cm (½in) of unsewn canvas for turning.

2. Cut out the cushion pieces as follows, using the Cutting Plan (*fig.1*) as a guide. Cut out the cushion back, adding 10cm (4in) to the size of the needlepoint from top to bottom and 15cm (6in) from side to side. This allows for the fabric border around the needlepoint. A 1.2cm (½in) turning has been allowed for all seams except for the zip seam which has a 2.5cm (1in) turning.

fig. 1

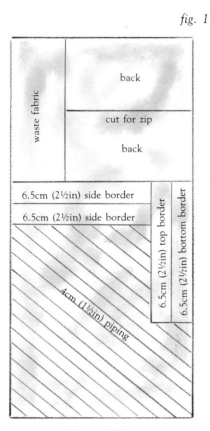

Cutting Plan

3. Cut four borders 6.5cm (2½in) wide and 15cm (6in) longer than the size of the needlepoint.
4. Cut piping strips 4cm (1½in) wide on the bias. Sew the piping strips together (*fig.2*). Press seams open and trim off projecting points.

fig. 2

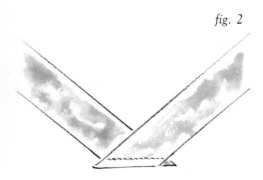

5. Fold the backing fabric in half from side to side and cut along the crease to form the zip opening. Sew in the zip as for the cushion with the twisted cord trim on page 140, taking 2.5cm (1in) turnings.
6. Next make up the fabric border. To do this, pin the top border on to the front of the canvas, right sides up, overlapping the finished needlepoint by 1.2cm (½in). Fold the fabric under at each end to form a mitre and press a crease (*fig.3*). Repeat with the other three border strips. Tack and machine the mitres along the creases. Trim away excess fabric, leaving 1.2cm (½in) turnings. Press open.

fig. 3

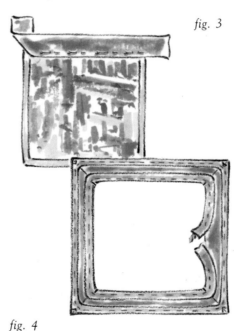

fig. 4

7. Make up a length of piping by folding the piping strip in half around the cord and machining in place using a piping foot. Leave a short length at each end open for the final joining of the piping. Attach the piping to the border as follows. Tack it into place around the right side of the border, with 1.2cm (½in) turnings (*fig.4*), clipping the piping strip at the corners. Neaten at the join as in *fig. 5*.
8. Tack and machine the piped border to the edge of the needlepoint, right sides together, clipping corners. Make sure that the mitres are positioned exactly at the corners of the needlepoint.

fig. 5

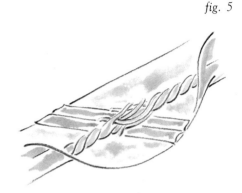

9. Tack cushion back to cushion front, machine and then double stitch or overlock the seams. Turn to the right side through the zip opening.

* * *

SQUARE BOXED CUSHION WITH PIPING

Materials

0.5m (⅝yd) fabric 122cm (48in) wide
Zip 8cm (3in) shorter than height of finished cushion
Piping cord No.3 to fit twice around the gusset
Pins

1. Stretch the needlepoint back to its original shape and cut away any excess canvas, leaving 1.2cm (½in) of unsewn canvas for turning.
2. Cut out the cushion backing to the same size as the canvas, adding 5cm (2in) to the width measurement for the zip seam. Fold the fabric in half from side to side and cut along the crease to form the zip opening. Sew in the zip as for the cushion with the twisted cord trim on page 140, taking 2.5cm (1in) turnings.
3. Cut four gusset pieces 8cm (3in) wide and the length of the sides of the canvas including turnings. As a precautionary measure, size each border separately (in case the canvas sides are slightly different in length) by laying it right side to right side of the needlepoint and cutting away any excess fabric protruding over the canvas.
4. Cut piping strips 4cm (1½in) wide on the bias. Make up a length of piping as for the cushion with the mitred fabric border (left).

5. Pin or tack the top gusset to the side gussets and the bottom gusset to the sides, taking 1.2cm (½in) turnings.

6. Notch the cushion front at the bottom, and also the bottom gusset. Machine the gusset seams together to make a ring.

7. Pipe the gusset all round along both edges, taking 1.2cm (½in) turnings.

8. Tack the gusset all round the needlepoint cushion front, right sides together, matching the notches on the bottom edge. Clip gusset seams to turn the corners. Then tack the cushion backing to the gusset. Machine and then double stitch or overlock the seams. Turn to the right side through the zip opening.

* * *

CURTAIN TIE-BACKS

Materials

For each tie back:
0.7m (¾yd) buckram,
    45cm (18in) wide
0.3m (⅜yd) interlining or bump,
    90cm (36in) wide
0.3m (⅜yd) lining fabric, 90cm (36in)
    wide
0.5m (⅝yd) fabric for frill (optional)
Twisted cord (optional) 10cm (4in)
    longer than measurement around
    the tie-back
Two rings
Pins

1. Take a pattern of the needlepoint tie-back after stretching it back to its original shape. Cut out the buckram using the pattern.

2. Rub a damp cloth over the buckram and iron on the bump/interlining. Cut off excess bump to the edge of the buckram.

3. Trim away the excess canvas from around the needlepoint, leaving 2.5cm (1in) of unsewn canvas all around for turning. Place the bump to the wrong side of the needlepoint and pin around. The finished needlepoint should come to the edge of the buckram.

4. Turn the tie-back over and clip around the canvas turning. Dampen the buckram, fold the turning to the back and iron the turning to the buckram.

5. If using a cord trimming, sew it on at this stage. Alternative trimmings may be used, such as piping or a pleated frill with piping.

6. Cut out the lining 1.2cm (½in) bigger than the finished work. With wrong sides together, pin to the tie-back, folding in the turnings and clipping where necessary. Slipstitch the lining to the needlepoint.

7. Sew on the rings at the ends of the tie-back just inside the cord, positioning one on the needlepoint side and one at the opposite end on the back of the tie-back.

* * *

ROUND STOOL COVER

The instructions given are for the type of stool obtainable through needlework stockists and as supplied by Glorafilia. For an antique stool or variations, adapt these instructions.

Materials

Stool 28cm (11in) in diameter
Strong thread

Tapestry needle
1cm (⅜in) upholstery tacks

1. After the design has been stretched back into shape, thread a tapestry needle with a length of strong thread and work running stitches around the canvas about 2cm (¾in) outside the needlepoint circle to form a drawstring.

2. Place the needlepoint face down on a table and centre the padded stool top on to the needlepoint with base upwards. Ask someone to place their hand in the centre of the base and press downwards. Then pull both ends of the drawstring, drawing the canvas edges over the base; tie firmly with a bow. Ease out the gathers to obtain an even finish around the edges.

3. Leave the top for one or two days to allow the canvas to stretch, then make final adjustments, easing out the gathers again if necessary.

4. Now tack the canvas to the underside of the base with upholstery tacks, 1.2cm (½in) from the edge and 1.2–2cm (½–¾in) apart. Trim off surplus canvas with scissors or a craft knife 2cm (¾in) from the edge.

5. Place the padded top into the stool base, turn upside down and twist the screw or tighten as indicated.

* * *

EVENING BAG

Materials

0.5m (⅝yd) lining fabric,
    90cm (36in) wide
Pins

1. Stretch the needlepoint back to its original shape and cut away any excess canvas, leaving 1.2cm (½in) of unsewn canvas for turning.

2. Cut the lining to the same size as your work, including the unsewn canvas. Place right sides together and tack, leaving a 8cm (3in) opening down one side. Machine around the edge. Trim away the corners; this will help to make flat corners when the bag is turned to the right side.

3. Turn to the right side through the opening and press flat with a warm

iron. Neaten the opening.

4. Working from the right side of the needlepoint, sew the sides of the bag together with small stitches, using grey stranded cotton. Fix a stud to close, adding a tassel if you wish (see Tassels below).

* * *

MIRROR FRAME

This is not an easy project. We suggest that you take the completed mirror frame to a framer for a professional finish. However, if you are adventurous and have lots of patience, go ahead.

Materials

Hardboard panel approx. 28cm (11in) square and 3mm (⅛in) thick (check measurement of your work first)

Photo-frame strut back the same size as hardboard panel (obtainable from a frame maker)

2 strips of 3mm (⅛in) thickness hardboard measuring 28×8cm (11×3⅛in), and 2 strips measuring 12×8cm (4¾×3⅛in)

Mirror glass 12cm (4¾in) square and 3mm (⅛in) thick

About 28cm (11in) square foam sponge 1cm (⅜in) thick

Copydex or similar adhesive

Bulldog clips

Paper or fabric tape in suitable colour

4 turnbuttons (from a frame maker)

Felt tip marker in a matching colour

1. Stretch the canvas back into shape. Using a felt tip marker in a matching colour, stain the canvas to a width of about 1.2cm (½in) from all needlepoint edges. (This prevents white edges of canvas showing on the finished frame.)

2. Mark out and cut the hardboard panel 3mm (⅛in) smaller all round than the sewn needlepoint, with a central square opening 3mm (⅛in) larger all round than the centre of the needlepoint. Bevel the inside and outside edges. Using a suitable adhesive, cover the face of the panel with foam sponge. Bevel the edges of the sponge with a sharp knife (*fig. 1*).

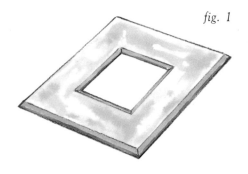

fig. 1

3. Before mounting, trim the excess canvas to about 2.5cm (1in) all round and cut the corners as in *fig.2*. Place the needlepoint over the hardboard panel. Glue the back of the panel

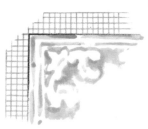

fig. 2

and fold the canvas around it. (Avoid gluing any part of the cotton yarn of the needlepoint.) Start with two opposite sides, then the other two sides. Work the needlepoint edge to the panel edge and use bulldog clips to hold the canvas in position until set.

4. With a sharp knife or scissors, cut the unsewn canvas in the centre as shown in *fig.3*. Glue the canvas on to the back of the hardboard panel using the same procedure as before. Trim the excess canvas.

fig. 3

5. Take the photo-frame strut back and glue on the strips of hardboard at the top, bottom and two side edges. The strips should be

positioned to leave an opening 12cm (4¾in) square for the mirror (*fig.4*).

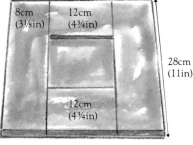

fig. 4

28cm (11in)

8cm (3⅛in) 12cm (4¾in)

28cm (11in)

12cm (4¾in)

6. Bind the raw edges of the strut back with a suitably coloured paper or fabric tape. For a professional finish, cover the whole back and edges including the strut leg with coloured paper. Position the mirror within the hardboard strips and hold in place with turnbuttons.

7. Finally, glue the needlepoint-covered panel and the strut back together. Hold together with bulldog clips until completely set.

* * *

TASSELS

This is just a guide. To vary the size of the tassels, just add or take away strands of yarn or cut them to different lengths.

1. For each tassel cut 12 strands of left-over yarn approximately 75cm (30in) long. Fold in half and in half again. This will make a chunky tassel approximately 10cm (4in) long.

2. Take a strand of yarn, make a slip knot around the tassel and wrap the strand around the centre two or three times. Make a loop with the excess strand of yarn. Then make three crochet chains from the loop, leaving the yarn intact to sew on to the finished item.

3. Fold the tassel in half at the chain. Wrap another strand of yarn around it several times, 1.2cm (½in) down from the top of the tassel. Finish off securely.

4. Cut through the loops at the bottom of the tassel and trim ends evenly. Sew on to the cushion or bag where required.

1. TENT STITCH

TENT stitch, which forms a fine background of short slanting stitches, can be worked in a number of different ways.

CONTINENTAL TENT stitch (A) is worked *horizontally* across the canvas. Work from right to left. At the end of the row, turn the canvas upside down and work the next row, again from right to left. In REVERSED TENT stitch (B), the stitches simply slant in the other direction.

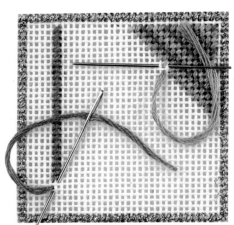

VERTICAL TENT stitch should only be used for single *vertical* lines, e.g. outlining. BASKETWEAVE is worked *diagonally* from the top right-hand corner without turning the canvas. This is the best stitch to use on larger areas of background as it does not distort the canvas as CONTINENTAL tends to.

2. CHAIN STITCH

When CHAIN stitch is worked in close rows, it makes a texture rather like knitting. Work vertically from the top down. To make a horizontal row, give the canvas a quarter turn so that the top is at the side, then work the row vertically.

To begin a row, bring the thread through at the top (A) and, holding the thread down with your left thumb, insert the needle into the same hole and bring it out two canvas threads lower down. Keeping the thread under the needle, pull the needle through the loop.

To continue, hold the thread down with your thumb, put the needle into the same hole (B) and bring it out two canvas threads down. With thread under needle, pull the needle through the loop. To finish a row, work a tiny straight stitch into the same hole to anchor the loop. Work rows two canvas threads apart.

3. SATIN STITCH

This is an easy and versatile stitch, good for "filling-in" and wonderful in borders as numerous different patterns can be formed. It is also the basis for many other stitches.

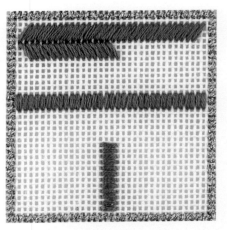

SATIN stitch is made up of straight stitches set close together. Here the stitches are shown first worked diagonally in both directions, then worked vertically and then horizontally.

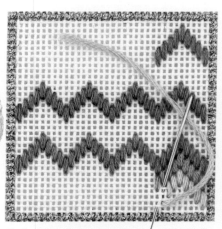

To build up this zigzag pattern, work the first row vertically from right to left over three canvas threads. Add rows of varying shades to follow the line of the first.

SATIN STITCH

A variation of SATIN stitch is shown here to fill in a flower. The flower has a BACK stitch outline and stem (see below).

The SATIN stitches radiate out from the centre. Two or more shades can be used.

4. BACK STITCH

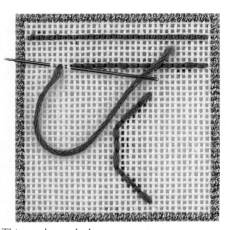

This can be worked over one, two or more canvas threads. It makes longer stitches on the back of the canvas than on the front. It is useful for outlining as it can turn corners.

5. FRENCH KNOTS

FRENCH KNOTS can be worked singly or clustered together as above. They are very useful when working flowers, as they are perfect for stamens or flower centres. The FRENCH KNOTS in this flower have been outlined with SPLIT BACK stitch (see below).

Bring the thread through to the front and twist it around the needle two, three or four times depending on the size of the knot. Then put the needle down in an adjacent hole, anchoring the twist with your thumb.

6. SPLIT BACK STITCH

Similar to BACK stitch, this stitch gives a finer, more fluid look, especially when working stems, leaf veins or outlines. Bring the needle down through the middle of the previous stitch.

7. LONG & SHORT STITCH

LONG AND SHORT stitch is a form of SATIN stitch more commonly used in embroidery. It is so called due to the varying lengths of the stitches. It is useful on areas too large or irregular to be covered by SATIN stitch – perfect for flower petals as it can follow each curve. The stalk is in STEM stitch.

In the first row of LONG AND SHORT stitch, the stitches are alternately long and short and follow the outline. The stitches in the following rows are of similar lengths and fit in to the previous row. For a smoother effect, split the thread of the previous stitch.

8. STEM STITCH

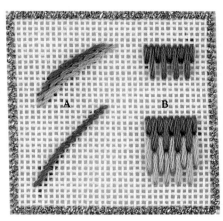

STEM stitch (A) is useful for flower stems or outlining. Work from left to right following the guideline, using stitches of a similar length. Each stitch overlaps the previous one. LONG AND SHORT stitch (B) is shown here worked vertically in regular rows.

9. CROSS STITCH

CROSS stitch is one of the easiest and most popular stitches, perfect for beginners. It looks as good on a small-gauge canvas as on a large canvas and is very hard-wearing.

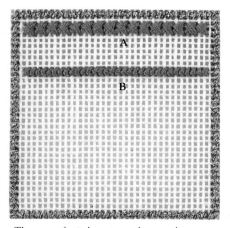

The row of stitches (A) at the top shows CROSS stitch worked over two threads of canvas. The next row (B) shows the stitch worked over one thread.

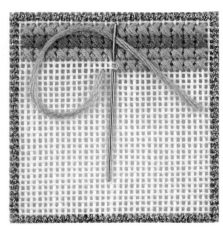

CROSS stitch is worked from right to left. At the end of the first row, turn the canvas and continue working from right to left. Complete each cross before beginning the next one. It is not important which way you cross as long as all the upper crosses lie in the same direction.

10. DOUBLE CROSS STITCH

DOUBLE CROSS stitch is a bold stitch with a raised texture and it looks very attractive when worked in two or more colours.

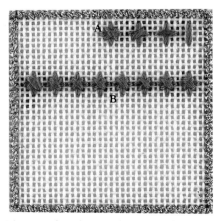

The row of stitching at the top (A) shows, from right to left, how the stitch is built up. It consists of a straight cross over four canvas threads with a diagonal cross over two threads worked over it. Work the first row horizontally from right to left (B).

The rows of DOUBLE CROSS stitch interlock as shown above. When you reach the end of the first row, sew the next from left to right without turning the canvas.

11. SCOTTISH STITCH

SCOTTISH stitch is an extremely useful background stitch, whether it is worked in different colours or in alternate directions in the same shade.

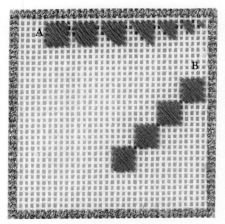

The stitch is built up from seven satin stitches worked diagonally to form a square (A). Work the squares diagonally downwards for the first row (B). It may be easier to give the canvas a quarter turn to work the second row diagonally upwards.

Alternate rows of a pale and a dark shade are worked in SCOTTISH stitch diagonally to give a chequerboard effect.

12. BRICK STITCH

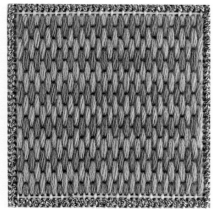

BRICK stitch consists of a series of straight stitches taken over two or four canvas threads and laid in staggered rows like bricks. The stitch can be worked horizontally or vertically, and makes an excellent background stitch.

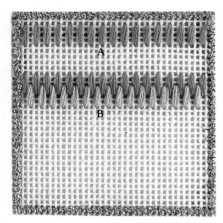

The top line of stitching (A) shows how each row is worked over four threads of canvas with a space of two threads in between. The lower line of stitching (B) shows how the next row begins two threads lower down and the stitches interlock neatly.

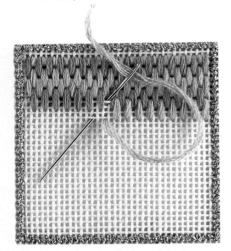

Work the first row from right to left, the second row from left to right, and so on. Do not turn the canvas.

13. CONTINUOUS MOSAIC

CONTINUOUS MOSAIC stitch is an interesting background stitch which gives the impression of woven straw.

The stitch is worked in diagonal rows which can slant either from right to left or from left to right as you wish.

Work the stitch diagonally over one and two threads of canvas. The second row butts up to the first – the small stitch interlocks neatly with the larger stitch. Do not pull the thread tightly as this will distort the canvas. Work rows alternately upwards and downwards.

14. HUNGARIAN STITCH

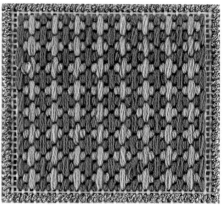

HUNGARIAN stitch looks particularly striking when alternate rows are worked in different colours as here, although it gives an interesting texture when worked in a single colour.

The stitch consists of a unit of three straight stitches worked in horizontal rows. The first stitch of the unit is worked over two threads, the second over four, and the third over two, as shown above (A). A space of two threads is left before beginning the next unit (B).

Work the first row from left to right, then work the second from right to left. Continue in this way, with each row interlocking with the preceding one.

TASSELS
Project on page 22

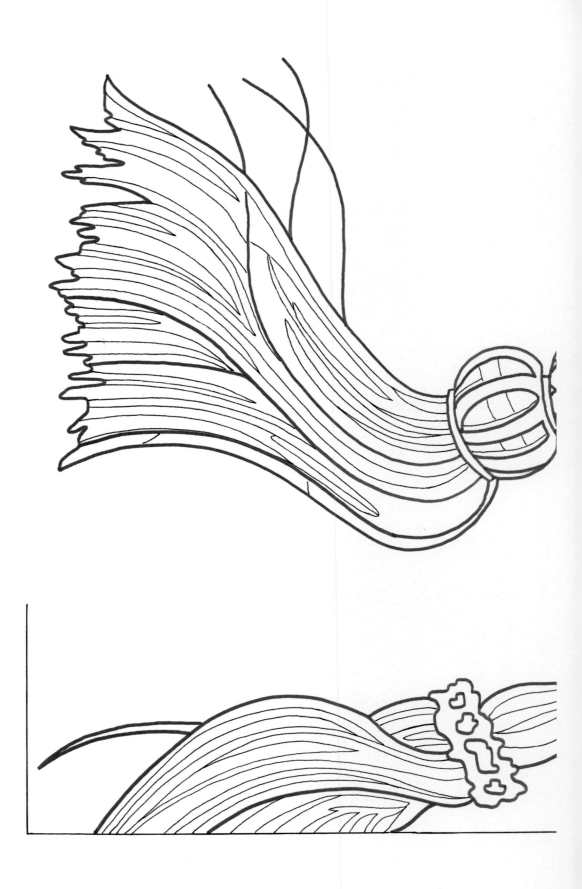

TOP

CORRER
Project on page 46

YELLOW PANEL Project on page 18

CA' REZZONICO STOOL
Project on page 54

SHELLS
Project on page 80

FRUIT PLACEMAT AND NAPKIN
Project on page 91

PIERROT
Project on page 102

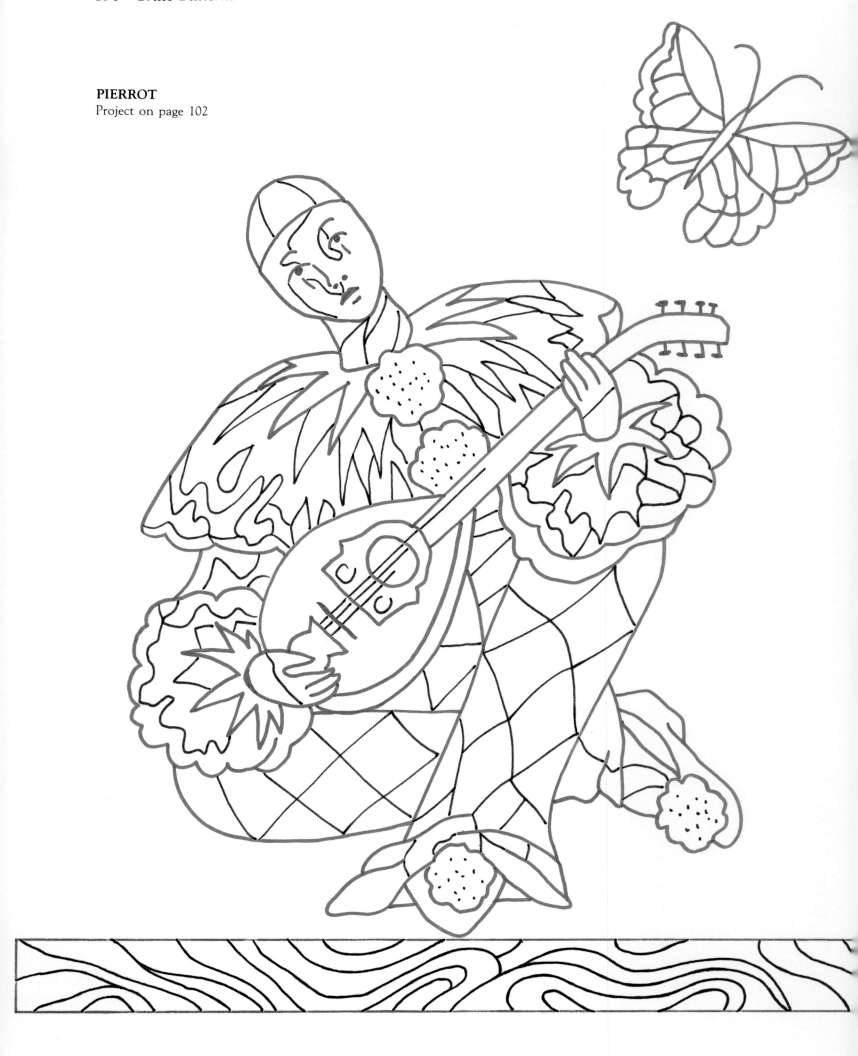

PAROCHET FRAGMENT
Project on page 32

With thanks to: Maggie Pearlstine, cheerleader extraordinaire; and to all at Conran Octopus for their wonderful enthusiasm, especially Mary Evans, whose smile didn't even falter when the tapestries were impounded at Venice Airport. To Bill Batten for his nothing-short-of-exquisite photographs; to Ian Rooks who shared our passionate view of the city. To our Glorafilia girls, particularly Daphne King and Shirlee Sharpe, and the greatly gifted Ros Neale, Julie Baldwin and Djien

Bishop; to Sorel, who now counts squares in her sleep; to the Ladies Who Sew: Lynda Blundell, Mary Clark, Andrea Cooper, Dorothy de Lacy, Vicki Henley, Chris Gregory, Judy Hart, Joyce Talbot and Barbara Williams.

To our families and friends for being so understanding and neglected – did you miss us? And, of course, to Venice herself. In a world of uncertainties and unthinkables, long may she survive.

The publisher would like to thank the following for supplying materials for photography:
The Gallery of Antique Costume and Textiles, London NW8; Judy Greenwood Antiques, London SW6; Peter Hurford Antiques, London SW6; Indoor Garden Room, Stratton Audley, Oxfordshire; Paul Jones, London SW3; The Lacy Gallery, London W11; McKinney Kidston, London SW6; Sylvia Napier Antiques, London SW6; Keith Skeel Antiques, London N1. pp 24–5 Background and floor painted by Matthew Lauder.

Materials and kits service

Glorafilia can provide all the materials needed to complete each project in this book: canvas cut to size and taped at the edges, the correct needles and enough yarn to complete the design, and various items of equipment that you may need.

The following designs are also available as kits. They each contain canvas printed in full colour, instructions, needles and all the necessary yarns.

Complete kits
Tassels, p 22
Correr, p 46
Ca' Rezzonico, p 54
Geraniums, p 62
Fruit Urn, p 84
Pierrot, p 102
Mandolin and Mask, p 112
Venetian Bridges, p 112
Lace, p 122
Marbled Cushion, p 132

If you would like to receive further information, or order kits or materials directly, write to: Glorafilia Ltd, The Old Mill House, The Ridgeway, Mill Hill Village, London NW7 4EB. Tel: 081 906 0212. Fax: 081 959 6253.

Useful addresses
Cords and tassels
Distinctive Trimming Co, 17 Kensington Church Street, London W8 4LF.
Tel: 071 937 6174.
Cushion and stool making
Glorafilia Ltd, The Old Mill House, The Ridgeway, London NW7 4EB.
Tel: 081 906 0212.
Fabric suppliers
Designers Guild, 271/277 Kings Road, London SW3 5EN. Tel: 071 351 5775.
H.A. Percheron Ltd (distributors of Rubelli fabrics), 97 Cleveland Street, London W1P 5PN. Tel: 071 580 1192.
Arthur Sanderson & Sons Ltd, 53 Berners St, London W1P 3AD. Tel: 071 636 7800.
Framers
Masterframes, 857 Honeypot Lane, Stanmore, Middx. Tel: 081 952 2664.
John Tanous Ltd, 115 Harwood Road, London SW6 4QL. Tel: 071 736 7999.

Yarn suppliers
For details of stockists and mail order sources of the yarns used in this book, please contact the following addresses:
Anchor yarns, Astrella metallic thread, Penelope lurex thread
Coats Leisure Crafts Group Ltd, 39 Durham Street, Glasgow G41 1BS. Tel: 041 427 5311.
Coats Semco, 8a George Street, Sandringham, Victoria 3191, Australia.
Tel: 010 613 5981011.
Appleton's yarns
Appleton Bros. Ltd, Thames Works, Church Street, Chiswick, London W4 2PE.
Tel: 081 994 0711.
Clifton H. Joseph & Son Ltd, 391/393 Little Lonsdale Street, Melbourne, Victoria 3000, Australia. Tel: 03 602 1222.
DMC yarns
DMC Creative World Ltd, Pullman Road, Wigston, Leicester LE8 2DY. Tel: 0533 811040.
DMC Needlecraft Pty, 99–101 Lakemba Street, PO Box 131, Belmore 2192, N.S.W., Australia. Tel: 010 612 5993088.
Madeira metallic thread
Madeira Threads (UK) Ltd, Thirsk Industrial Park, York Road, Thirsk, North Yorkshire YO7 3BX. Tel: 0845 524880.
Penguin Threads Pty Ltd, 25–27 Izett Street, Prahran, Victoria 3181, Australia.
Tel: 03 529 4400.

Picture credits
The publisher thanks the following photographers and organizations for their kind permission to reproduce the photographs in this book:
5 *top* Bridgeman Art Library (Christie's, London); 5 *above left* Graziano Arici; 5 *above right* Jacqui Hurst; 5 *centre left* Marka (Loris Barbazza); 5 *centre right* Susan Griggs Agency (Horst Munzig); 5 *below left* Agence Top (F le Diascorn); 5 *below right* Spink & Son Ltd; 6 *above left* Tony Stone Worldwide (Michelle Garrett); 6 *below left* Michael Holford; 6 *above right* Impact Photos (Mark Cator); 6 *below right* Sarah Quill/Venice Picture Library; 7 *above left* Michael Holford; 7 *below left* Graziano Arici; 7 *above right* Susan Griggs Agency (Adam Woolfitt); 7 *below right* John Heseltine; 10 *above right* Zefa Picture Library; 11 Marka (Loris Barbazza); 12 *above left* The Bridgeman Art Library (Galleria degli Uffizi, Florence); 12 *below left* Reale Fotografia Giacomelli (Museo Correr); 12 *above right* Museo Fortuny (Emanuela Girardello); 12 *below right* Soprintendenza per i Beni Artistici e Storici; 13 *above left* Osvaldo Böhm; 13 *below left* Scala, Florence (Ca' Rezzonico); 13 *above right* Graziano Arici; 13 *below right* Osvaldo Böhm; 14 *right* Graziano Arici; 15 *above* Scala, Florence (Accademia, Venice); 15 *below* Reale Fotografia Giacomelli (Museo Correr); 16 *above* Reale Fotografia Giacomelli (Museo Correr); 16 *below* Scala, Florence (Accademia, Venice); 29

Communita Ebraica di Venezia; 34 *above left* Susan Griggs Agency (Adam Woolfitt); 34 *below left* Cent Idées/Mahn; 34 *above right* Cent Idées/Mahn; 34 *below right* Sarah Quill/Venice Picture Library; 35 *above left* Guy Bouchet; 35 *below left* Agence Top (Laurence Vidal); 35 *above right* Marka (Loris Barbazza); 35 *below right* Glorafilia; 36 Courtesy of Chris Beetles, St James', London; 37 Marka (Loris Barbazza); 45 Reale Fotografia Giacomelli (Museo Correr); 48 *above left* Guy Bouchet; 48 *above right* Sarah Quill/Venice Picture Library; 48 *below* Guy Bouchet; 56 *above left* Susan Griggs Agency (Adam Woolfitt); 56 *below left* Tony Stone Worldwide; 56 *above right* Bridgeman Art Library (National Gallery, London); 56 *below right* Agence Top (F le Diascorn); 57 *above left* Explorer (Samuel Costa); 57 *below left* John Heseltine; 57 *above right* Susan Griggs Agency (Adam Woolfitt); 57 *below right* Marka (Loris Barbazza); 58 Tony Stone Worldwide (Michelle Garrett); 66 *above* Marka (Loris Barbazza); 70 *above left* John Heseltine; 70 *above right* Sarah Quill/Venice Picture Library; 70 *centre* Hutchison Library (Bernard Régent); 70 *below* Marka (Loris Barbazza); 74 *above left* Graziano Arici; 74 *below left* John Heseltine; 74 *right* Graziano Arici; 75 *left* Graziano Arici; 75 *above right* Marka (Loris Barbazza); 75 *below right* Jacqui Hurst; 76 *above* Jacqui Hurst; 76 *centre* Graziano Arici; 76 *below* Jacqui Hurst; 94 *above left* Giraudon (Galleria dell'Accademia Carrara); 94 *above right* Impact Photos (Mark Cator); 94 *below left* Marka (Loris Barbazza); 94 *below right* Susan Griggs Agency (Horst Munzig); 95 *above left* Impact Photos (Mark Cator); 95 *below left* Impact Photos (Mike McQueen); 95 *above right* Giraudon (Palais Rezzonico); 95 *below right* Impact Photos (Mark Cator); 96 Impact Photos (Mark Cator); 98 E. T. Archive; 106–107 Mary Evans Picture Library; 116 *above left* Marca (Loris Barbazza); 116 *below right* Jesurum; 117 *above left* Glorafilia; 117 *above right* Jacqui Hurst; 117 *below left* Spink & Son Ltd; 117 *below right* Graziano Arici; 118 Jesurum; 120 Susan Griggs Agency (Adam Woolfitt); 121 Tony Stone Worldwide; 124 Totem Gallery.

Chapter side panels
Introduction: Bridgeman Art Library (Christie's, London); *Venetian Textiles*: Graziano Arici; *Decorative Venice*: Marka (Loris Barbazza); *Backstreets and Backwaters*: Agence Top (F Le Diascorn); *Venice and Food*: Jacqui Hurst; *Carnival*: Susan Griggs Agency (Horst Munzig); *Crafts and Characters*: Spink and Son Ltd.

The following photographs were taken specially for Conran Octopus by:
Bill Batten 1, 2, 3, 17, 20, 21, 24–25, 26, 30–31, 38, 40, 44, 49, 52–53, 60–61, 65, 67, 71, 78–79, 82–83, 87, 90, 97, 99, 104–105, 108–109, 112, 116 below left, 119, 125, 129, 130–131, 134–135.
David Gill 9, 18, 22, 27, 32, 39, 41, 43, 46, 51, 54, 62, 66 below, 68, 72, 77, 80, 84, 88, 91, 100, 102, 110, 113, 122, 126, 132, 136, 144–147.